The Secret Landscapes

lara Brack

lara Brack was born in Melbourne in 1949, the first of four aughters of artists Helen Maudsley and John Brack. After an rts degree at Melbourne University, she taught in Technical chools and then TAFE. She also wrote and took photographs, aking books for family and friends. In 2014, she self-published *he Eye Sees Not Itself*. *The Secret Landscapes* is the result of ver twenty years of writing releasing herself from inhibitions bout putting her story into a public place.

Clara Brack

The Secret Landscapes

On Not Pleasing your Mother

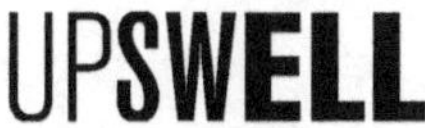

st published in Australia in 2026
Upswell Publishing
rth, Western Australia
swellpublishing.com

swell operates in the city of Perth, on ancient country of the Whadjuk
ople of the Noongar nation who remain the spiritual and cultural
stodians of this beautiful land. We acknowledge their continuing
nection to country and express gratitude to elders past and present for
ir strength and creativity…Always was, always will be, Aboriginal land.

N: 978-1-7642397-3-8

A catalogue record for this
book is available from the
National Library of Australia

ver design by Chil3, Fremantle
peset in Foundry Origin by Lasertype
nted by Lightning Source

swell Publishing is assisted by the State of Western Australia
ough its funding program for arts and culture.

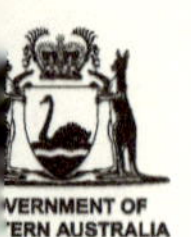

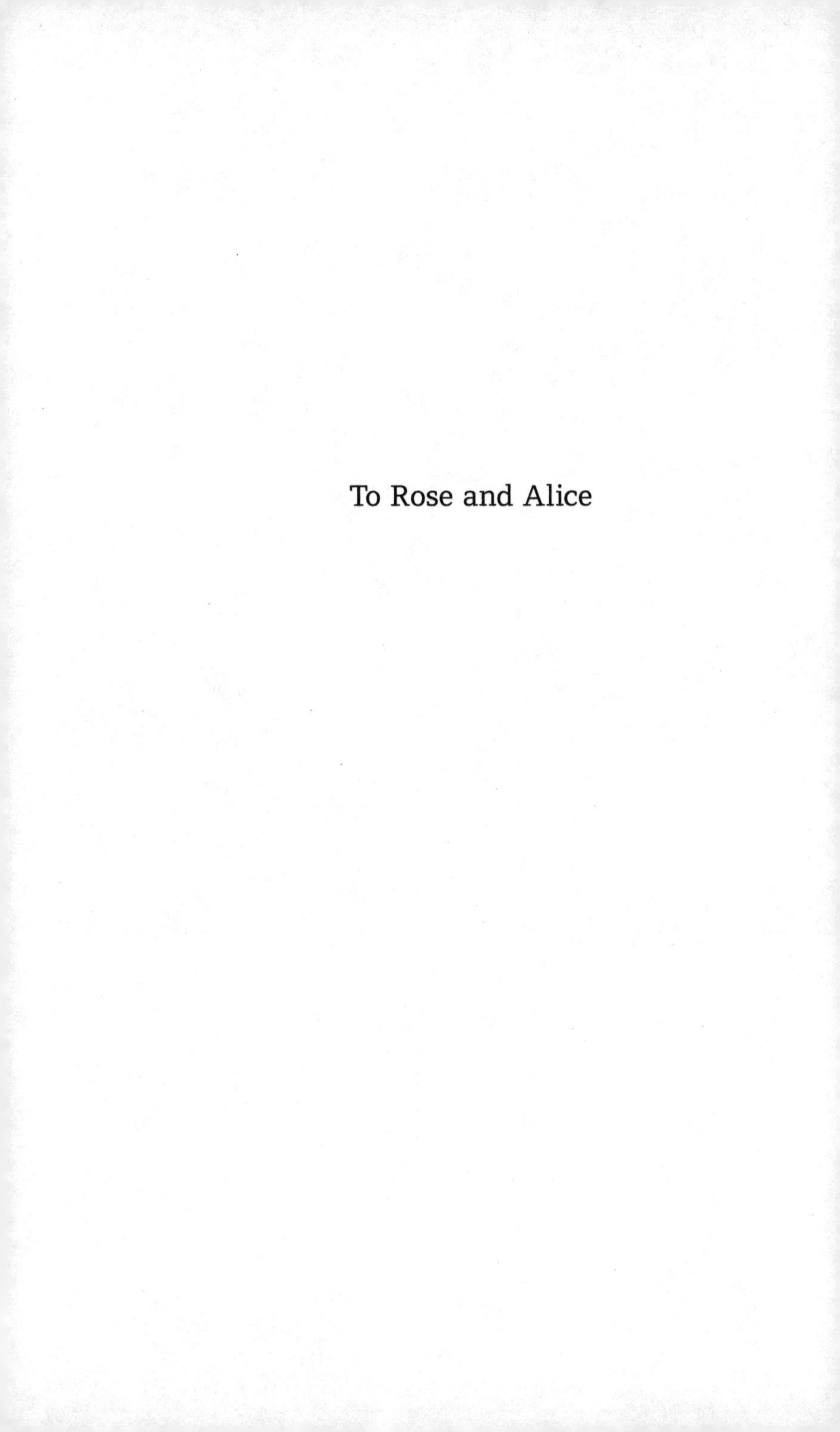

To Rose and Alice

Art is theft, art is armed robbery, art is not pleasing your mother.

Janet Malcolm

Introduction

My parents are artists John Brack and Helen Maudsley. They m at art school and exhibited their work in Melbourne from the 195 for fifty years. My father was born in 1920, my mother in 1927. M father's work was well known. School students wrote essays on h painting *Collins St 5pm.* When asked if my father was John Brack would sometimes say, 'My mother's an artist, too. Helen Maudsle 'Oh is she? I don't know her work, never heard of her.'

'Why don't you write a book about your parents?' a friend on asked me, knowing that I wrote books for family and friends. Sask Grishin had written a book about Dad's work. A book proposed c Mum's work never eventuated. I imagined that after Mum's dea a 'real' writer would do some research, interview artists and frien look at the paintings, read what my parents had said and writt about their work, and then come up with an engaging account their lives together, of how his work was well known but hers wasn It would tell the story of two artists in a formative time of Austr ian art.

I imagined that the real writer would face the usual obstacles writing a biography, exacerbated and enriched by it being a doub biography. I imagined they would be free of the struggles I faced wi my own writing. I was envious of the expertise of this writer despi the fact that this accomplished book existed only in my imaginatio hen the real writer had finished this book, he or she would move ıto the next while I would still be puddling along in the margins .ving been interviewed for that one.

There is one significant difference between me and this imaginary riter, apart from the fact of never having published a book. I have en shaped by my parents, by the relationship between them. If I ere to write a book, I would make this part of the subject. I would plore the obstacles that inhibited my writing—my father's voice in e, 'you dill', and my mother's 'private is private' which, for many ars, swamped my capacity to imagine or to allow myself to find my vn voice.

There are also the gifts. The gift of being brought up in a home with iginal paintings on the walls, of seeing the inner life of my parents their paintings, of the encouragement to make things, to invent, break from convention. The gift of seeing the illusoriness of fame ıd what it takes to resist it. The gift of knowing the tenacity and the scipline required to continue working despite negative reviews and tle interest in the work. The gift of knowing that art is simply hours ıd hours in the studio working alone.

There are the gifts and then there is the legacy we carry.

If I were to write such a book, how would I start? I would art by describing an experience that the 'real' writer would not ce—the disjunction between the artist as a parent and the artist in eir work.

*

ım in an art gallery looking at a painting. It's a fresco. It depicts landscape draped with a piece of folded fabric reminiscent of e Renaissance masters. The sea shimmers with the hint of gold. The esco radiates a mysterious tranquillity unlike any of the paintings grew up with. I want to buy it but the man I need to see is speaking on the phone. He ignores me. Since I was brought up not to interru the important man, I do not interrupt him. I look around the galle waiting for him to finish speaking, but I am not prepared to ha around any longer, hoping to avoid the peak-hour journey home.

The next day I ring the gallery and tell the man that I want to bu the fresco. I give him my name and the numbers on the credit card.

'Are you any relation to John Brack?'

'He's my father.'

'Oh. He's my favourite Australian artist. I love *Collins Street 5p* I love the pictures of the postcards and the pencils.'

As he continues a glowing appraisal of my father's work, I visuali my father pacing the hallway of our family home, clenching his fis wrestling with himself in morose melancholy.

This man loved my father's work.

Others were not so enamoured. 'I can't imagine how you live wi that hanging on the wall.'

My parents' paintings formed the landscape of my childhood. Dad paintings were hung in the room visitors would enter, Mum's were the children's bedroom and in the hallway. Their paintings were n joyously spontaneous, paint flung onto the canvas haphazardly. Th were painted with meticulous control like the disciplined routine our household. When friends ask me, 'Do you like your parents' pai ings?' I mumble something about not being able to distinguish the paintings from my experience of the artists as my mother and father

When my mother saw the fresco I had bought, she looked at it for moment and then said, 'It doesn't have any conflict in it.'

She said it like a chef declaring that the meal was lacking salt. Sh seemed puzzled, suggesting that a work of art devoid of conflict ha no meaning to her. The absence of conflict may have been what dre me to the fresco. It is not 'cerebral' as Dad's paintings were known. is not 'serious' in the way that Mum defines 'serious'. It takes us in the natural world, the mystery, the unknown.

*

e friend who suggested writing a book on my parents had proposed write about 'what it was like watching your mother and father paint-g, how they got their ideas, the secrets, the funny stories, the affairs'.

'Have you ever looked at their paintings?' I thought to myself. 'Do u think a child of those artists would even consider writing this sort book?'

I understood the curiosity to know about the lives of the people lled 'artists'. The art is mysterious. A secret about the artist's life uld shed light on the mystery of the work. If we feel we know the tist in the work, we feel we are entitled to know about the person ho made the work. Furthermore, artists are given licence to step out-de the 'bourgeois' rules other people follow. The secrets, the affairs.

My mother and my father were adamant that the artist's work eaks for itself. Dad would repeat: 'Everything to know about me is in e paintings.' Mum would repeat: 'Private is private, public is public.' r both of them, the private life of the artist was out of bounds. esides, any artist would rather the interest was in the work, not the cret affair or what they got up to during the weekend. Nevertheless, was mystified by the vehemence of my mother's insistence 'private private'. As I saw it, there was nothing that warranted the urgency keep something secret. When Dad was not at work teaching, he as busy painting. Mum went into her painting room after we left for hool and reappeared when we returned. We had dinner the same me every night. We took our library books back on the due date. either my mother nor my father had the temperament to dance on e table and were far too responsible and dutiful to run off with other eople's husbands or wives. As Dad has said in an interview, 'Some eople would think of it as a boring life going into the studio day after ay, six days a week, but for me it is fulfilling.'

I found myself thinking, 'All right, I will write a book about th secrets, the affairs.' I would start the book with making my mothe visible but since few people knew of her work, I would surrender t starting with what the reader would know: a story about my father.

My Father

I would give my father a secret life. He would have a lover. I wou call her Sonya. He would meet her on the train. He will ask her wh she is reading. She will be reading *Anna Karenina* in Russian. Dad w entranced by the Ballets Russes when it came to Melbourne wh he was eighteen. Sonya will have defected from the Ballets Russ She will work as a translator commuting to the city from a cotta in the country. My father will visit her every second weekend. O day during lunch he will complain about not having a studio. Son will turn towards the window, wave her fork and say, 'Why don't y paint landscapes?'

If the writing were to have meaning for me it would have to ha a purpose. It would have to fulfil some need in me. It would have be inspired by my curiosity rather than answering to someone els needs.

I am one of four daughters. Clara, Vicky, Freda and Charlotte. V sometimes speculated on what it would be like if there was a boy our family. This was my opportunity to find out. My father will ha a son with Sonya. He will stop seeing his son after the ending of t affair. He will leave the landscape paintings in Sonya's house. One his landscape paintings will be on the cover of the book.

The son will not commit suicide as my mother predicted when v speculated on having a boy in our family. 'He could never live up hn's expectations.' In his early twenties, the son will seek out the ther he never knew. My father will write letters responding to his n's questions about his parents, the son's grandparents, about how became an artist, about his paintings.

One morning I found myself embarking on writing the letters my ther wrote to the son he never had.

As the letters progressed, I put aside the obstacles until I could no nger avoid them. For the very reason that my father did not have this cret life, I could not imagine it. It was beyond what I knew of him. It as inconceivable that he would have a lover. The fantasy of his secret e demanded that I exceed the limits of the suspension of disbelief.

I abandoned the idea for what it was—a provocative response a suggestion to write a book about 'the secrets, the funny stories, e affairs'.

*

'ead that John Brack had 'bravely stopped painting having said all at he wanted to say'. I understood that he had stopped painting cause periodically the paintbrush slipped from his hand. Mum had cked his studio and hidden the keys to prevent him from continuing s attempts to 'improve' his paintings.

He had dementia from alcoholism.

A few years later he died, aged seventy-nine.

When Dad was first diagnosed with dementia, Mum became his rer. She performed this task with amazing fortitude and dedication it also with understandable resentment. To give her a break I offered take him away for three hours on Sunday afternoons. He had ouble walking and did not like to be near other people, so I opted for drive in the country. Dad had once painted a picture called *The Car*, picture of a father and mother in the front seat, a boy and a girl in e back looking out the window. The trees through the car window

suggest that they are driving in the country. For most of my childho
we didn't have a car. Now we were belatedly doing what other famili
did, this time with the daughter driving.

In the attempts at 'conversation', I asked Dad about painting. Son
times he was lucid, revealing little snippets I doubt he would ha
revealed were it not for the dementia.

'Helen has taken all my money. She has put it into her bank accou
She has taken it, you know, because I am successful and she is n
I feel sorry for Helen. She did not get the recognition she deserves b
she paints in her own private language. She's an artist's artist. Sl
works so hard, you know. She is very, very serious about her work
am successful and she is not. So, that's why I haven't any money no

Sometimes on our walks he stopped and looked at me in terror. 'W
have to go home. She will be so angry with me. I don't know wh
I have done wrong.'

At the time I assumed it was Mum who would be 'so angry'. Lat
I wondered whether it may have been his mother.

After returning him safely, I felt the disappointment of not gettir
what I had secretly hoped for: some meaningful connection. I ha
rarely spent more than two or three hours with my father alone. I
the time I was permitted three hours, he had lost his mind.

'Do you have any regrets?' I asked him on one of the drives, hopir
he would say, 'I wish I spent more time with you children.'

'I wish I had painted with more confidence like Picasso.'

My anger was palpable. I wish I had lived with more confidence
myself, like those whose fathers said, 'well done'. I remember thinkir
'I could stop the car, open the door, push him out and keep driving.' I
would offer no resistance.

Once, when we had ended up at Shoreham Maze, we walked ba
and forth getting lost as one does in a maze, and as I shepherde
him out, the thought came to me, 'I could leave him here and dri
off.' I pictured the newspaper headline, 'Artist found lost in maz

um would be livid. If I told her that I had wished to push him out ' the car she would have said, 'How could you think such murderous ıoughts?' She must have had her own. She had more reason to than lid.

One Sunday I brought the camera with me, intending to take Dad's ıotograph, recalling the series of photographs that Richard Avedon ok of his dying father. I stopped the car at a walking track. I took ıe camera out of the bag and slung it over my shoulder. 'I'll take the ıoto on the way back,' I said to myself. As we returned from the walk paused before getting into the car. 'I have to do it now,' I thought. I ırned and looked at my father. I stared at him, noting the position of ıe trees in the background, framing the photograph to ensure that tree wasn't growing out of his head. My hand clung to the camera my side, ready to raise it. I saw my father's bewildered confusion. heard my mother's voice, 'How dare you.' To take the photograph ould not only capture the image of his face but possibly also stir up a emory of the use of the camera. Dad posed cooperatively for photos, nstructing himself for the photographer. The sight of the camera ould elicit the thought that he had lost his former self. To take the hotograph would be to capture the moment his terror of this loss as ignited.

Driving back home, I recalled the impulse not to take the photo-raph. It was like taking a man into a secluded part of the country nd taking a gun to his head. 'Is this what happens when you plan murder?' I thought. When it comes to the point, you can't do it. he photo could only have been taken if I had been able to resist my other's voice: 'How dare you.' It could only have been taken if I had ot imagined the terror that taking the photograph would induce in man who had lost his mind and was vaguely aware of the use of ıe camera.

Although the photo was not taken, I can now re-create in memory ıe photograph I did not take.

It is black and white. An old man is looking at the camera. His eye are watery, vacant. He is looking at the photographer in dazed puzzl ment. His skin is blotched, marked with little tributary veins. Hi mouth is closed but not quite closed as if he is about to speak. His ha is unkempt. Something is missing. There is no angst, no depression, n self-loathing, no struggling with himself. He is not self-consciousl posing for the photo, aware of the relationship to the photographe He is a ghost of himself.

I like to think that it was not my mother's voice, 'How dare you', th stopped me from taking a photograph of my father. It was compassio

*

Whenever I saw Dad, I put my thoughts and feelings on hold. I deferre to him. I entered his territory, asking him questions about art. I wa fearful of his criticism, but I also wished to protect him. Deeply withi him one sensed a vulnerability, a fragility, a void. It felt to me that sense of dark precariousness hung over the family, exuding an om nousness that could never be referred to. I was not aware of it until left home. I knew very little about Dad's childhood. I knew that he wa estranged from his parents and that they lived not far from us. I didn know their names. I knew that they had to leave school at twelve an thirteen as *their* parents could not afford to keep them at school. O the rare times Dad spoke of them, he emphasised that it wasn't the fault they didn't have an education.

Twice in my life I had occasion to refer to his parents. The first tim I was sixteen. The phone rang soon after I got home from school.

'Is John there?'

'No, I am sorry he's not. Can I give him a message?'

'Tell him his mother rang.'

'Yes, I will Mrs Brack.'

She hung up. Moments later, I realised I had been speaking to y grandmother. Something had given me the presence of mind to olitely call her 'Mrs Brack'. I remember preparing myself to tell my ather, as if nervously going to speak to the headmaster. I waited until e was sitting alone in the sitting room. I went in.

'Daddy, your mother rang.' His head fell. 'She would like you to ng her.'

'Mmph,' he mumbled, looking at the floor. I tiptoed out. Message eceived.

We never spoke of Dad's parents. We never thought of them. It was s if they existed in some other place. When Mum matter-of-factly old me that Dad's father had died, I wanted Dad to know that I knew is father had died. *He* was *my* father. He must have felt something bout the death of his father. I had to consider how to tell him. I could ot say, 'I know your father has died.' That would sound accusing. I felt pang of nervousness as I heard myself saying respectfully, 'Daddy, am sorry to hear that your father died.' His head fell, his eyes looked own at the table. Silence. I refused to break the silence. 'Hmph,' he runted. I had done something more invasive than knocking on the oor of the studio and interrupting the important man. I had crossed ne threshold of what was permissible to speak.

I had never seen a photograph of Dad's parents until the gathering after his funeral. It was then that Uncle Lindsay gave me three hotographs—a photo of Dad as a young man, a photo of their father nd a photo of their mother sitting on a seat with her two sons. In the hoto with their mother, Dad looks about ten. Lindsay would be eight. ad's head is inclined towards his mother, his arm around her back. is mother's head is inclined towards him. Lindsay sits on the other ide of his mother, sitting straight up looking at the camera. I like to elieve there was a time when Dad loved his mother and she loved im. The evidence is there in the photograph. The son's arm around is mother's back, their heads inclined towards each other.

The thought came to me: what if my father could find the lo that I saw in that photograph of the boy with his mother? What if I made some connection with his parents? What if Dad *did* put dov his paintbrush 'having said all that he wanted to say'? What if I stopped drinking? What if he didn't get dementia? What if he had a alternative ending to his life?

An alcoholic friend of my father's had fallen into the gutter after a afternoon and evening drinking in a pub. He was found by a passer- and taken to hospital and then sent to another hospital to dry out. I went to AA and resurrected his career, avoiding the dementia th would have been his fate had he continued drinking.

What if I 'gave' this story to my father?

I could not imagine my father having a lover, but I could imagi him falling into the gutter, drunk. I could imagine him agreeing stop drinking under the threat that if he didn't, he would get deme tia. I could not imagine him sitting in a room with strangers talki about their drinking in meetings of AA. If he were to give up the gr I would need to find an alternative to AA. Drinking was not a hobl It was self-medication, an attempt at dealing with the torment of h life. I would have to find some other means for understanding wh troubled him.

*

Something had troubled me.

For several months every night I woke up recalling a conflict wi my boss. Night after night I replayed what he had said, what I had sa what he had said, how he had tricked me into agreeing to a meeti where he humiliated me in front of my colleagues.

I went to see a psychotherapist.

Instead of telling her what had happened with my boss I four myself telling her about an incident with my father.

'My father has dementia. He was in hospital having a prostate eration. He thought he was in a hotel. When I visited him, he had his ck to me, washing his hands.

'"Hello Daddy," I said.

'He turned his face towards me, beaming. "I'm so glad to see you."

'He had never said he was glad to see me.

'"I'm so glad you're here. I didn't know how I could get home. I ven't got any money for a taxi. I thought I could ring Freda and ask r for some money, but I couldn't do that. It would be *abject*. It is *ject* for a parent to ask a child for money."

'I wanted my father to be pleased to see me.

'If it is abject for a parent to ask a child for money, it is even more ject for a father to lose his mind, especially a man known for his telligence. "I am a cerebral painter," he said when asked what sort of inter he was. If I had been humiliated by the meeting called by my ss, he would have been even more humiliated had he known that he d lost his mind to dementia. Clambering for the dignity of his former lf, he told me and the nurse taking his blood pressure, "See that nd-basin over there. I made that. I won first prize in a competition."

In the sessions with the psychotherapist, I discovered what had unted me about the incident with my boss.

I began to wonder what would happen if my father went to see a ychotherapist. A therapist would provide the space to explore the lf that required the self-medication. Dad preferred the intimacy of nversation with one trusted friend. It was beyond my suspension disbelief to imagine him visiting a lover in the country, but faced ith the choice between getting dementia and seeing a therapist, magine he would choose the therapist if there was no option to take s own life.

His sessions with a therapist would give me the opportunity to nderstand the origin of his torment. It would give me the opportunity find compassion for him and for him to find compassion for himself.

If I were to write his sessions with a psychotherapist, I would ha to overcome my mother's voice in me: 'Private is private'. In wonderi about the notion of the private becoming public I recalled an exchan between two characters in a novel by Patrick White. The man h received 'a highly coloured post-card' with 'snatches of informatio The woman has received a poem about a glacier. The man asks to re the poem. The woman replies, 'It's far too private, I mean, you on show your poem to those you want to see it—unless, of course, yo throw it wide open to the public.'

In throwing *this* wide open to the public, I draw on what my fath has said in interview and conversation, what he has written and wh I see looking at his paintings.

In his visits to the therapist Dad will speak about the person mo important to him, the person on whom he depended: his wife. Th reader will be introduced to my mother through the eyes of my fath In devising a scenario where my mother also speaks to a therapi I explore the origin of her fear of what would emerge if the priva was made known. I explore the relationship between her life and h paintings and her position in the world where the artist was assum to be a man. In speaking to her therapist about Dad, the reader w gain an insight into her relationship to him and how she ensured th his work took priority.

The title of the book, *The Secret Landscapes*, refers to the secre of my father's childhood. It refers to the secrets of my mother ar those passed on from her parents. Secrets take the form of inn landscapes. Through confronting my own impulse to secrecy I explo how secrecy infiltrates the works of the writer and the artist. Th subtitle, *On Not Pleasing Your Mother*, is from Janet Malcolm, wh suggests that art is subversive, challenging the boundaries of what permissible: 'Art is theft, art is armed robbery, art is not pleasing yo mother'. My father defied his mother in choosing to be an artist, m mother defied her mother in her marriage to an artist, and in writi hat my mother considered private I am defying her. In doing so I ffer what she yearned for.

In earlier drafts, overshadowed by my mother's voice, 'private is rivate', Dad refers to Mum as 'Hilda'. In emerging from the shadow f the private, I gave my mother her real name. I refer to my father as ad' although I never called him 'Dad', I called him 'Daddy'. Mum tells e that he called his parents 'Mother' and 'Pater'. She referred to them s 'Mr and Mrs Brack'.

I have called the therapists T and V as if they are real people wishing to maintain their anonymity.

Sessions with T

How would I actually get Dad to the sessions with the psychotherapist? Mum would have to drive him. On the way there he says, 'I don't know why I am going to see this fellow. I haven't done anything wrong.'

Mum: Look, it has been so much effort getting you off the grog. If you don't go, you will lose your mind with dementia. Do you want that? No. Well, I certainly don't. I don't fancy giving up my time to look after you.

Dad: I don't want to go.

Mum: You have to go and you have to do what the man says. And you have to say thank you when he's finished with you.

Dad: (*sarcastically*) Thank you, thank you, thank you.

He sits in the waiting room and then T arrives.

T: Welcome, John, come in. T indicates a chair.

As he sits down, Dad says: I'm only here because Helen says I have to be here. Apparently, you are rescuing me from dementia. Man to the rescue.

T: I am here to help you with what troubles you.

What troubles me goes into my paintings.

Long silence.

T: Just say whatever comes into your mind.

I am not the master of spontaneity. I am not the sort of artist who wakes up in the middle of the night declaring, 'I'll paint the moonlight

T: You are not here as an artist, you are here as a human being, a 'oubled human being.

My troubles go into my paintings. That's where they're hidden, if ou care to find them.

T: It is said that 'the artist is like a child playing a sophisticated ame of hide and seek. It is a joy to be hidden but a disaster not to e found.'

It is not a joy to be hidden, it is a necessity.

T: It is our work to take you out of hiding.

What do you mean *our* work? I've never worked with anyone in my fe. The artist is a solitary being.

he statement, 'a joy to be hidden...' is from Donald Winnicott, a sychoanalyst. I am not pretending to be a psychoanalyst. The charac- er of T is a literary device to explore the hidden life of my father.

For the next six months Dad sits in silence for the duration of the fty minutes. T will make a brief comment at the beginning and ne end of each session. Eventually Dad will say to T what he said to ne during one of our drives in the country:

When I came home late from school, my mother hit me with my ather's belt. She said it was for playing with the lower-class boys in ne next street. I didn't know what I had done wrong. I thought we ere lower class.

T: Are you telling me that you don't know what you have done rong having to be here?

I don't know what I have done wrong. Every day I find myself etracing the steps of how I got to be here.

T: Tell me how you got to be here.

One morning Helen told me that she was going away to stay with er sister Emily for a few days. Her sister lived in the country. That vening, I came into the kitchen to heat up the dinner she had left for ne but when I turned on the light a paralysing melancholy came over me. The simple act of turning on the light reminded me that Helen w not home. She usually set the table which meant that even getting t knife and fork felt onerous to me. I barely managed to eat the dinn she had cooked and then, after washing the plate, I poured mys more whiskey and stumbled into the sitting room where I turned the television. I must have dozed off. I remember waking, fearful th something had happened to Helen and she would never return. I w ried about not having enough whiskey in the house despite knowin bottle was concealed under the leaves surrounding the bay tree.

I got up and walked out of the house towards the bottle shop, fu aware that the shop would be closed. I can only imagine that my wir had got crossed and in my deranged panic I thought that if the bot shop was open Helen would return. I arrived at the darkened sh knowingly defeated. Each step on returning home brought me clos to the emptiness of the house, to the despair that there would be no ing more to paint, to the worry that my memory was failing me.

As I stepped from the footpath onto the road, I tripped headlo into the gutter. Instinctively, I thrust out my arm to protect me but I landed on the concrete, a fierce spasm of pain wracked through m arm. I had no will to get up. There was nothing I could do but succum to lying sprawled where I had tripped. In silent resignation I clos my eyes like a child who imagines that if he closes his eyes no one ca see him.

Here I am at the still point of the turning world, I said to myself. F the first time in my life, I had no fear of falling, no sense that som thing would topple over. I had fallen.

So this is it! I said to myself, as a man might declare gazing at th view from the summit of the mountain he had climbed. So this is it, th still point of the turning world. I found myself dozing in and out sleep beyond caring what would happen to me.

I woke startled by a man's voice saying, 'My God, what's happen to you, mate?'

The voice was unfamiliar but then after a slap on the face I heard, ake up. Wake up.'

Obediently I opened one eye and then closed it.

'Blood shot,' the man said, offering his layman's diagnosis. 'I'll get ambulance. What's your name, mate?'

'Blood Shot,' I mumbled.

Were it not for the stranger who found me, I may never have rived at the hospital. I would never have been told to stop drinking.

T: And now you are here.

And now I am here.

I wrote that account, I could almost convince myself that Dad had llen in the gutter and was rescued by a passer-by. I was giving my ther an alternative ending to his life. He was coming alive on the ge in dialogue with T. I was speaking as a ventriloquist in the voice my father.

*

the next session he says:

Mother's quest for me and my younger brother Lindsay was to get t of the working class. I knew that if we were to enter the middle ass, we would have to do something about our accents which would ve us away. Every day for three months Lindsay and I listened to e wireless and practised speaking in the voice of the ABC radio nouncers who, in those days, spoke in the accent of the upper-class itish man. There! I have told you something about myself. Twenty ars after Mother hit me for playing with the lower-class boys in e next street, I married an upper-class girl from the other side of e river.

Mum would never have married Dad if he had not taught himself speak in the accent of the ABC radio announcers. She told me about exhibition opening. 'And there was [name of artist] speaking in th dreadful working-class accent. There he was going yob yob yob.'

He says to T:

No one knows the effort for the child of working-class parents invent himself as a middle-class man.

T: Do you want to tell me the effort?

I want to tell you how I studied what was specifically required the artist in Australia in the twentieth century. No artist is truly ori nal. The evolution of any artist's work is very largely a recapitulati of the art of the past. One learns how to paint by studying the gre masters and as the artist moves slowly and painfully towards findi his own schema, he becomes aware that each of his paintings cou be titled 'Homage to…' I came to the discovery that if I painted in t recognisable style of the European masters but took life in the Austr ian suburbs as the subject of the painting, the work would contribu to shaping our identity and therefore my own identity as an artist.

T: You are giving me insight into your work as an artist. Is this a g I am privileged to receive or is this a means to distract us?

The artist is his work. I was in it for the long haul. And now the lo haul is over.

T: The artist may well be his work. This is our work exploring t inner life of the man who constructed the persona of the middle-cla man that demanded so much effort. We are in this for the long haul.

*

In the next session he tells T:

My father left school when he was twelve years old. It was t Depression. He worked in the brewery. Mother left school at thirte ıd learnt to sew as a milliner and dressmaker. I have one brother, ndsay, who is two years younger than I am.

Mother expected us to do very well at school, to 'pull the family ıt of poverty' as if 'poverty' was a well we had to be pulled out from. :other had something more invested in me than simply earning a ecent living. In her mind I was destined to be a genius. She expected 'eat things from me. It pleased me to please her with my good marks. :other's praise made me feel indestructible.

One of my earliest memories is of Mother taking me and Lindsay to ıe toy shop to select the present from Father Christmas. My eyes fell ı a model of a German howitzer gun. I knew that it cost more than :other could afford and therefore beyond what we were permitted. looked at it avidly, picked it up and studied how it worked while ndsay contented himself with looking at the lead soldiers within :other's price range.

On Christmas day it delighted me to see that Father Christmas ad given me the toy I had found irresistible. In compensation that ndsay had not received such an exotic toy, I allowed him to play ith it whenever he wanted. I once carved him a realistic automatic stol from a solid piece of wood.

T: You are telling me that you discovered that your mother would ake concessions to you that she did not make for your brother.

There were other concessions. She had taken us to buy new coats hich she had heard were on special. When we arrived at the shop, ıe veered us towards a table tumbling with coats. She poked her hand ıto the thriving mass and extracted a coat which she held against me. ıe dull purple left me aghast. I refused to try it on leaving Mother to ersuade Lindsay to try on the coat she had selected while I looked at rack of garments not marked down on special.

Lindsay and I walked out wearing our new acquisitions, he resigned the indignity of purple and me in respectable navy blue. On the way ome we called in to visit Aunty Ethel. Mother explained we had been shopping for new coats. Aunty Ethel looked at each of us appraisingl 'What good taste John has,' she said.

T: You discovered that your mother made sacrifices for you.

As I said, Mother saw me as special. I remember my embarras ment when I overheard her reading out my report card to Aunty Iv 'They're just marks. What's all the fuss?' Aunty Ivy said, refusing t respond as was expected of her. It was then that I knew that the goo marks were for Mother. Mother was claiming my 'success' as her ow It was like the shock of discovering that your mother isn't really you mother, she is someone else.

Mother's anger when I said I wanted to go to the art school co firmed that her praise was only forthcoming if I did what was expecte of me. It wasn't my success she wanted. She wanted my success fo herself. I wanted to tell her, 'We have to be separate. A mother can live through her son. You have to find your own meaning in life.'

T: It was a wound for both of you when the honeymoon was over.

I doubt that T would say that, but that is the sentence that wrote itsel

If Mother saw me as special, Pater saw me as his accomplice. He woul take me by the hand and say, 'Let's ask Mother, shall we.' He liked t keep the peace. He was easily intimidated. It wasn't his fault he had t leave school at twelve years old.

I remember the moment I realised my father's inadequacy. I wa ten years old. He had taken me and Lindsay to the museum on Sunda afternoon. As we huddled over the exhibits, my father read aloud th sign next to the glass cabinet, even though we were capable of readin it ourselves. I stood idly looking on, distracted by another father a the neighbouring exhibit. The other father was not reading the sig he was explaining the exhibit in his own words, responding to th questions his children asked, elaborating.

As we waited at the bus stop, Pater attempted to engage me in con-ersation, reporting a fact about one of the exhibits we had seen. He ad confused one exhibit with another. Fuelled by my disappointment ı him, I did something I had never done before.

'No, you're wrong,' I said. 'Don't you know that? Don't you know nything?'

My father raised his hand as if shielding his eyes from the sun. He ıay have intended to slap me but then thought the better of it. As is hand covered his eyes, the shame of my father burned through ıe. My brother witnessed the little fire knowing it was I who had lit ıe match.

T: You had humiliated your father for not being the sort of father ou would have liked.

And you are not the sort of psychotherapist I would have liked. here must be others better than you. I don't even know who you are. know nothing about you. Helen's father was a psychiatrist. Before oming to see you I'd never even heard of a 'psychotherapist'. Besides, ow can any of us understand another person, let alone ourselves?

T: We are all ordinary human beings. We are all mortal, the Nobel rize winner, the cashier in the supermarket, the man who collects the ickets on the tram. We are all interconnected. We are all connected to he trees, the stars, the animals of this world. If we look at it this way ur hearts can be healed.

What makes you think that little statement will make any differ-nce to me?

T: A little statement like a poem or a painting can wait for us. It is here to recall when we are receptive to it.

What is the point of any of this? I give up. I am leaving.

He leaves before the end of the session.

f Dad didn't want to hear something, he would get up and walk out f the room, supposedly to get more whiskey and more ice. You would hear the iceblocks being extracted from the aluminium iceblock tr and then the occasional cursing as the iceblocks danced onto the flo

*

In the next session he says:

You are right. I had humiliated my father for not being the sort father I would have liked. I was probably not the sort of son that would have liked.

Inadvertently I once humiliated Mother. I had got a scholarship Ivanhoe Grammar. A school uniform was required. As I tried on t jumper, the blazer and the long pants, Mother looked on admiring Uniforms impressed her. She had been led to believe that the sch would pay for the uniform as part of the scholarship. This proved n to be the case. She could not afford to pay for the uniform. The sour of her hope and pride was now the source of her profound disappoi ment. I had done my part in getting the scholarship to go to the priva school. She had not done her part in buying the uniform to go the I could not take up the scholarship.

T: You felt you had inadvertently humiliated your mother.

It wasn't my fault, but I felt protective of Mother. I did not blan her that I could not take up the scholarship. She was more dis pointed than I was.

After I left school at fifteen and a half, I got a job in an insuran office in the city. If it were not for a chance encounter one day aft work, I may never have become an artist. I was passing a shop in Litt Collins Street when I saw amongst the clutter in the window tv coloured reproductions of paintings by Van Gogh. I was overco with shuddering and a shiver in the spine. The thought came to me, painting could do that, I could do that.' The torment of the soul cou express itself in something as mundane as a bed and a chair in t swirling of the paint.

T: It was an epiphany.

It was an epiphany. I will never forget that shudder of recognition. ıad a purpose in life. The next year I enrolled in night classes at the llery art school. A year later I saw for the first time an unfinished ·zanne landscape. Again, I was overcome by a shuddering, a tingling the spine. The painting was speaking to me even more directly than e Van Gogh which I had only seen in reproduction. I knew someing in that moment although I could not articulate what I knew. The ıinting had lifted me out of the drab suburban ordinariness of the 30s. If Cézanne and Van Gogh could do that, I could do that.

I had to postpone my classes at the gallery school in 1940 when I rned twenty and enlisted in the army. The six years in the army proded no opportunity to paint or to have contact with other painters the night classes had. In those years between twenty and twen-five, the artist makes vital decisions based on how he interprets e work of his elders. He sees himself continuing a lineage based on s interpretation of what has come before. I never wanted to join an t movement. This may have been because I spent those formative ars alone without contact with other artists. Fortunately, it suited y temperament not to belong.

T: So instead of bemoaning what you missed out on in those six ars in the army, you saw what you had gained.

Exactly.

The time in the army was my first time away from home. My ırents kept in touch through disappointing letters. It is not that I pected Dostoevsky. I could hardly complain about the inadequacy of eir letters to me as my letters to them were no less mundane. I would ention a humorous little incident of no consequence whatsoever. It ay have been my references to the promotions that led to Mother's nviction that she would eventually become the mother of a general the army.

When I returned home after six years, I was no longer the naï twenty-year-old youth who had thought of himself as a man. It w disconcerting to notice that the furniture in the house was arrang just as it was when I left. I sat in the same chair at the kitchen tab Mother was only interested in one thing: what I was going to 'do' my life. When I told her I intended enrolling full time in the art scho she responded with, 'What do you want to do that for?' She had hop that my time in the army would rid me of my 'little hobby' and I wou agree to the more reputable career she had in mind for me.

As I ate my dinner, I pictured myself getting up and leaving th table, the room, the house and never returning. I didn't know wha was doing there, and yet there was nowhere else to go. I knew I wou have to keep living at home until I could earn enough money to pa the rent for a place of my own.

After dinner I sat on my bed and closed my eyes thinking, 'Everythi is just the same. Everything is dead like a museum.' I wanted to shal some sense into Mother: 'A parent can't live through the child. Each us must find our own meaning in life. Can't you get that into your f head. Don't you understand. I want to be an artist.'

It wasn't Mother's fault she missed out on an education, but I c not know what stopped her from getting a job. She had trained as milliner so there was nothing to stop her getting a job making her litt hats. She was an expert at sewing dresses. That wasn't good enoug for her. She wanted her son to be important, to do something in th world, not, as she saw it, getting out of proper work, dabbling wi pencils and paints.

The next day I walked along the street churning with fury Mother, wrestling with anger at my father for not defending me, cas gating myself for having the audacity to hope that my parents wou affirm what I wanted to do in my life. I kept walking with nowhe to go until I found myself walking through the open gates of the Ke emetery. I made my way towards a gravestone, put my head in my ands and burst into tears. Where else is one permitted to weep but in graveyard? I wept for the wretched pitifulness that everything was st the same. I wept for my own stupidity in having imagined that it ould be different. I wept for the futility of the deaths I had witnessed the army. I didn't care that Mother would see me as a sook. What d she know? She didn't know what had happened in the army.

T: You discovered that you could weep without admonishing your-elf for 'being a sook', defying your mother.

And when I stood up, I felt that I had been restored to myself. In is newfound lightness of being I picked up a faded pink plastic car-ation lying on the pathway and manoeuvred it into my buttonhole. 'hen I arrived home just in time for dinner Mother asked me where had been. 'I've been to a wedding. My own wedding. I'm married to rainbow.'

ad could not weep in the presence of his mother. I could not think in is presence.

'Did you see me in the newspaper?' I asked him, pointing to a photo-raph of hundreds of runners about to start a marathon. He had no terest in sport. At school you could either be good at sport or good at our work. We were expected to be good at our work.

'I ran twenty-five miles, forty-two kilometres.'

He looked at the photo. 'What did you want to do that for?'

It did not occur to me to say, 'Isn't that what your mother said hen you told her you wanted to be an artist?'

I could not think in the presence of my father. He may have felt the ame about being in the presence of his father and his mother.

*

He says to T:

My father was a defeated man. I, too, was defeated time and tim again. I had originally wanted to be a poet, but my attempts at poetr had failed. Words would always defeat me. Years later when I rea that Cézanne had said, 'I have failed to realise my sensations', I unde stood that the artist's sense of defeat does not necessarily arise fro the limits of his talent, it arises in all artists and writers. One is alway working at the limits of one's intelligence. The work never lives up t the ideal, the fantasy of its original conception.

Dad said he originally wanted to be a poet. He read a lot. He was ver particular with words. When I visited for lunch with my four-year-ol and two-year-old, he would place his *Oxford English Dictionary* o a chair, raising the height of the chair like a cushion. During lunc he would ask the four-year-old the meaning of 'obstreperous', 'dilap dated', 'euphemism'.

*

He says to T:

As an art student, on Sunday afternoons I looked at paintings in th art gallery. One late afternoon, I stepped out into the street overcom with a sense of dislocation as if my body had separated itself fro me. I assumed it was my eyes adjusting to the sunlight away from th intensity of the paintings I had seen in the art gallery, but the feelin persisted until I arrived at a park. The autumn light cast shadow on the green lawn. Mothers, fathers and grandparents were walkin with children. Single men and women were strolling alone. Couple reclined on the grass. Three or four boys were kicking a football. A I took in the scene, I found myself composing the tableau before m as a painting. The painting I constructed in my mind was an echo o Seurat's *A Sunday Afternoon on the Island of La Grand Jatte*.

The people in Seurat's painting were more grandly dressed. The adies were holding parasols, but the effect was the same. They were *njoying* themselves on Sunday afternoon. They were 'at leisure'. They were together as families. 'Leisure' sent me into moments of existential error. There was something I should be doing. I should be painting. I ave never longed for a 'pleasant' Sunday afternoon walking in the ark, strolling with the family. I needed the solitude to think about ainting, keeping a connection to the current work if I was not in the tudio working.

T: You are telling me that painting did something with the existen-al terror that you should be *doing* something.

I should be doing something now. I should be painting. I don't know why I am here. Why am I telling you this? I don't know anything about ou. For all I know, you could have poisoned your mother and thrown er down the well. Look at you with your Persian carpet, the books on ne bookshelf, the fancy lampshade, the dark-green velvet chairs. You now nothing about poverty.

T: I cannot know your experience of poverty if you do not tell me what it is. I can only go on what you tell me.

*

n the next session he notices a vase of daffodils in T's room. At the ight of the daffodils, he recalls William Wordsworth's poem. He starts y saying:

I wandered lonely as a child
That floats on high o'er vales and hills,
When all at once I saw a crowd,
A host, of golden daffodils;
Beside the lake, beneath the trees,
Fluttering and dancing in the breeze.

T: Did you hear what you just said?

I wandered lonely as a cloud that floats...

T: You said, 'I wandered lonely as a child.' Were you a lonely chil

I had no friends. There was no other boy I was drawn to and if a boy made a move to befriend me, I was ignorant of the move. I w wandering in my childhood. I had no idea of what I wanted to do in r life. I just knew I did not want to do what my father did.

T: You had no friends.

I will always remember meeting the man who would become r first friend. I was twenty when I went into the army. As I removed r books out of my bag, a hand grabbed one of them and a voice declar 'books', as if it was my teddy bear I had brought with me.

'Look what he's got. Books.' The pages were being flipped wher heard another voice declaring, 'Poetry!!'

I dared not look up and face my accusers. I feared the precio books would be ripped into shreds. Then I heard a voice saying, 'Gi them to me.' I looked up and to my astonishment the men relinquish the books. And so it was that in an army camp in Greta, New Sou Wales, I met John Stephens, my first friend.

T: This man rescued you from your initiation into the army.

He rescued me. I remember the first time we discussed Rilk *Letters to a Young Poet*. I had considered novels and poetry a sola but not something you could talk to with another human bei Stephens had been to university. He could converse about ideas, abo literature, about novels.

When Stephens returned from the army, he worked as a stockbrok in the city, but he suffered terrible guilt. Something had happened the army. His boss sent him to see 'the best psychiatrist in Melbour who, as Helen liked to remind me, was none other than her father. I married Joan and embarked on writing a novel which did not come fruition. He and Joan left Melbourne and bought a farm in Mittago New South Wales. Over the years, a tension emerged between I attributed this tension to the gap between my increasing success a ephens' failure to live up to his promise. It was Stephens who had me to my rescue that first night in the army. It was Stephens who d given me the benefits of his university education.

T: It was Stephens who had shown you the possibilities of friend-ip. What stopped you from speaking to me about Stephens before is?

I don't know. You tell me!

T: Stephens had come to your rescue in that humiliating initiation to the army. I had come to your rescue from losing your mind with mentia. If Stephens could fall apart, who is to say that I would t fall apart? If 'the best psychiatrist in Melbourne' could not help ephens, how could you trust that I would have any luck with you?

ad's last letters to John Stephens have been put into the National brary. They comment on the difficulties of painting, the deadline for exhibition, the negotiations with a gallery director. They end with ve my love to Joan'. I do not recall Dad being especially fond of Joan. may have been Stephens that he wanted to give his love to.

*

the next session he says:

I was able to enrol full time at the National Gallery art school under grant from the Commonwealth Rehabilitation Scheme. I was seven ars older than most of the other students who had come straight om school. Unlike them, I had no time to waste. When they chatted the breaks and at lunch time, I kept to myself.

One lunch time I was walking along the street when I noticed two the girl students coming towards me; one was a giggling dill and e other a more studious girl who stayed back for the night class. they passed, the dill clumsily made faces while the other looked nbarrassed. I ignored them.

Late that afternoon I was working on a drawing before the nig class. Nobody else was around. I heard the door to the studio open ar then looked up to see the embarrassed girl coming towards me. Wi out any introduction she said excitedly, 'Did you know that Seur used the same technique that we are being taught?'

I didn't know where she'd got that idea. 'No he didn't,' I said. 'Seur only used the pointillist technique.'

She showed me the book. I had to admit she was right. Then, wi out thinking, I heard myself suggest we have dinner before the nig class the next week. A week later I arrived where we had plann to meet, surprised to see that she was not alone. She was chatti to the student I had seen assiduously sketching in the portrait cla Freddy would be joining us for dinner. I thought he may have be her boyfriend, but when it became apparent that he wasn't, I w reassured.

I recalled the first time I had seen Freddy. One gloomy afternoon the gallery school I was doing a pastiche of Leonardo da Vinci wh I glanced up to see a young man entering the studio holding an armf of paper. He sat down and rapidly set about covering each sheet wi charcoal studies of the head of the model we were drawing. After few minutes, each sheet of paper turned into a black cloud which l then tossed impatiently onto the floor. What struck me instinctive was that while all of these studies failed to accomplish what I cou see he was aiming for, the attitude and the determination were tho of the first real artist I had ever encountered.

When I realised he would be joining Helen on our first outing, I w secretly overjoyed. A few months later Freddy confessed that wh Helen told him she was having dinner with 'that older rehab stude who keeps to himself' he suggested coming along as a chaperone. F the same reason I had wanted to meet him, he had wanted to meet m

Freddy and I shared a studio near the gallery school. We put a be in the studio so we could take shifts sleeping. It was our way of livi way from home. Although we were personally compatible, Freddy's ainting technique was somewhat different from my own. In his agerness to get at the paint, tubes of paint were simply chopped in alf. His painting procedure was frenetic. Frequently when the brush eemed too slow, the paint was applied impatiently, often desperately, ith a rag. Despite this, we had a similar approach to our work. Each f us felt the alienation of the artist but neither of us stooped to the ohemianism expected of an artist.

It was only once in my life that I ever felt cross with Freddy. I was eeting Helen for lunch. She had asked me to bring the petticoat she ad left in the studio. I was about to give up looking when a splash f pale pink caught my eye near Freddy's paintbrushes. I grabbed it, nowing instantly what had happened. Freddy had used it to wipe his aintbrushes. I would have done the same thing had I not recognised ne pink lying on the floor as a petticoat. It was Freddy who had ruined but, even so, I anticipated Helen's anger.

'Good Lord,' she said, examining the defaced garment I had returned. hat's just Freddy. He wouldn't have a clue. Mum bought that for me Georges.' In other words, it was expensive.

As I walked back to the studio, it occurred to me how easily I ad anticipated the anger of a woman. It was Mother's voice. It was lother's voice in me I could not escape.

T: It is our work together to understand this.

What do you mean, 'our work together'? It's not as if we are build-ng a sandcastle.

T: It is not just work we are doing. Maybe we are playing. Maybe e are making something together, something with the splendour of castle.

*

The next session he says:

I painted two portraits of Freddy. He painted two of me. I was more experienced portrait painter so his portraits of me were not a accomplished as mine. It was a mark of our friendship that he wa prepared to do my portrait on both occasions.

He struggled and struggled with the first portrait in 1950 until th canvas was encrusted with so many layers of paint it could almos stand up by itself. I do not know the fate of this struggle. Thirty year later he did another portrait of me. I am sitting on a chair in a jacke and a tie, ruddy faced, scowling, eyes averted, hands on my knee maintaining what little dignity I have. Darkness surrounds me. Fredd did not romanticise the troubled artist. He did not pretty up the imag of a friend. He saw the decrepitude I made no pretence to conceal.

T: You allowed Freddy to see you as you really are. You are allow ing me to see you as you really are.

In 1948, at twenty-eight, Dad drew a self-portrait depicting th self-conscious promise of the artist as a young man. In 1955, at th age of thirty-five, he painted a self-portrait as a confident, self-assure man. In 1972, at the age of fifty-two, he painted his body reflected i a shop window, outside looking in. It is not a self-portrait but it is th closest image of himself after painting the self-portraits. His head i concealed in the darkness of a shadow.

*

In the next session he says:

When Helen showed me the book on Seurat, she was just one c the girl students who had come straight from school. I knew very littl about girls. I had met Yvonne Lenny in the night class before going int the army and vaguely imagined that I might marry her until she tol me she was marrying a 'real artist'. The real artist was Arthur Boy 'ho came from a 'real artist' family. Briefly, I corresponded with Ruth 'ho I met before joining the army, but apart from that, my knowledge f women was non-existent.

Helen's upbringing could not have been more different than my wn. At fifteen I had left school to get a job to earn money. At fifteen, [elen was at St Catherine's private school with one tutor teaching er art and others teaching her the piano and the flute. She wanted ɔ leave school to go to the art school, but her father insisted she stay ɔ finish school. He then paid the art school fees as well as the fees for ıe conservatorium where she studied the flute. Before the war, the Iaudsley household was maintained by a cook, housekeeper, nurse, annies and a governess.

When Helen told me she was pregnant, it seemed inevitable that we rould live together, but given that her parents would never approve f us living together, one afternoon I found myself in Christ Church, outh Yarra, signing the marriage certificate with Helen's parents, my arents, Stephens and one or two friends.

T: You had to get married for the approval of Helen's parents.

Not only that, after my marriage to Helen, I discovered that it was bligatory to attend the Christmas afternoon tea at the home of her .unt Cecil. As we approached the imposing brick mansion, it seemed ɔ me we were entering another country.

We entered the dining room, confronted by a large oval table draped ı a white tablecloth covered with an array of scones, sandwiches and akes. I seated myself next to Helen as far from the head of the table s permissible. A woman wearing an extraordinary hat introduced erself as Nancy Adams. Her eccentricity seemed the only thing out of lace, apart from myself, and I was thankful for her exuberant chatter rhich meant that nothing was required of me except to listen.

As I glanced around the table, I thought I recognised an elderly entleman sitting next to Emily, Helen's sister. In that disconcerting pace between recognising someone and not knowing where one has met them, I half-heartedly listened to Mrs Adams, wondering whe I had seen this man before. It wasn't the army. It wasn't the art scho Then I was struck with a moment of recognition. His photograph w hanging in the lobby of the insurance office where I worked aft leaving school. It was L.F. Miller, the managing director. Nobody my department had ever set eyes on L.F. Miller. I could not understa what he was doing sitting at the same table as I was. What was I doing there? A figure from my past, albeit in a framed photogra had been inserted into what was already a discomfiting scenario. N one else seemed to notice the incongruity. I remember manoeuvri a chocolate éclair around the plate like a toy car, wondering how I got to be there. In what felt like an emergency, I could not put up n hand and ask permission to leave the room. The thought of making a escape reminded me that we would be required to perform the tedio ritual of shaking hands again before leaving.

Immediately we were out of earshot I asked Helen, 'What w L.F. Miller doing there?'

'He's my uncle.'

'What was he doing there?' I asked again.

'He's my uncle, Uncle Leo.'

I repeated the question, 'But what was he doing there?'

It took an effort of imagination to think of 'L.F. Miller' as the sam person as 'Uncle Leo'.

T: Could it be that in repeating the question, 'What was L.F. Mill doing there?' you were asking yourself the question, 'What was doing there?'

I am asking myself the question, 'What am I doing *here*?' I shou be in the studio painting.

*

ıe next session he tells T:

The afternoon tea at the home of Helen's aunt was followed by the deal of the Maudsley family Christmas dinner. Helen and I were the ungest people there. The others were the medical friends of Helen's ther. I remember sitting down at the long dining room table as the her guests found their places; unlike me, familiar with the ritual. ıe crisp white tablecloth had a decorousness lacking in the gingham oth we had at home. For something to do I picked up the circular ver napkin holder and noticed that it was engraved with someone's itials, presumably Helen's family. The formal magnificence unnerved e. I remember playing with a little sprig of holly, poking the prickled ges into my hand in a private flagellation.

During the dinner, the woman next to me asked the question I ould have anticipated, 'What do you do, John?' Her response was edictable. 'I've never met an artist before!' I felt like a rare species nging to escape to his own territory.

After the plum pudding the guests all stood up simultaneously. egan to follow Helen but my relief at departure was short-lived. It emed that the women adjourned to the sitting room while the men mained at the dining room table. Gloomily I returned to my chair, scouraged at the prospect of what was to follow. Gathering my nses, I succumbed to the port as the gentlemen launched into talking out the Great War as if picking up where they had left off from the st Christmas. I noticed Helen's father going to the sideboard collect-g the remaining knives, forks and spoons which he then placed on e table. The gentlemen then picked up these various knives, forks ıd spoons and used them to represent armies, replaying the battles om the Great War. I could imagine no greater discrepancy between e in the trenches and sitting drinking port in this grand mansion in uth Yarra.

*

Dad called Mum's father 'Sir'. I called him 'Fafa', an abbreviation grandfather. Every Saturday one of us children accompanied Mum the Prahran market. We took the tram to her mother's house and th Granny would drive us to the market in her car. We arrived at Mum parents' house as they were finishing breakfast. I remember o morning coming into the dining room and seeing the silver turee of stewed fruit, little silver toast rack, white table napkins. Fafa w sitting at the head of the table. He didn't say hello as he usually d He sat there, his head lowered.

I give this experience to my father:

As we got in the taxi to leave the Christmas dinner, I remembered th I had left my jacket hanging over the back of the dining room cha I sprinted up the Punt Road hill back to the house I had enthusias cally left moments before. I knocked on the door which was opened Helen's mother, who regarded me with her usual suspicion.

'I've left my jacket,' I said, intending to slip into the dining roo unnoticed. I stood in the doorway and looked in. Cigar and cigaret smoke swirled towards the high ceiling. The room was lit from th candles that continued to flicker in the silver candelabra. I was abo to make a move to collect my jacket when I noticed a figure conceal in the semi darkness. Helen's father sat alone, vacantly staring at th knives and forks that had collapsed after the battle re-enactments. H looked up in the realisation of one who has been discovered, tak off guard. He gave no sign of composing himself for an observer. N words were spoken between us as I collected my jacket and left th room. I recall a dark-red velvet curtain hanging over the window, backdrop to the smoky haziness in the candlelight, the man alo deep in contemplation. The scene bore the emotional resonance of Rembrandt painting.

T: What was the significance of this scene?

He knew and I knew in that moment that we both suffered from ›pression.

T: You had an affinity with your father-in-law that required no ords.

I must have passed a test for shortly after the Christmas dinner was offered a job as the art master at Melbourne Grammar. I had ɔ teaching qualifications. I had not done the fifth or the sixth form. understood that Dr Maudsley was friends with the headmaster ho was also a member of the Melbourne Club. Although not having ›plied for the job, I happily accepted as it was more lucrative than aming pictures and as it was only two days and two evenings a week, ıere was sufficient time for painting.

Dr Maudsley offered me another invitation, this time to join the [elbourne Club. In order to please him I found myself agreeing to go .ong to be introduced. Nothing could have been more alienating for ıe. I should not have put myself through this ordeal. The next day I rote a short, polite note declining the invitation.

Many years later we were called to Helen's parents' house, where ›r father lay dying. Helen was ushered upstairs into the bedroom here Emily and a few close friends had gathered while I was shown ıto the sitting room downstairs, wondering what was expected of me. nder the circumstances it did not seem appropriate to sit down and ıake myself at home, so I stood staring at a painting by Rupert Bunny. then gazed out the window, wondering if I had been forgotten or if I as supposed to be somewhere else. Just as I was wondering what to ɔ next, I heard the door opening. I turned and Helen came into the ›om. 'Dad died,' she said.

I burst into tears.

T: You felt grief for this man who understood you.

I never told him what he meant to me. He is there in *Collins St 5pm*. e is there indirectly in my magnum opus *The Battle*, a painting of the attle of Waterloo. The pens and pencils that represent armies take their origin from the knives and forks of the battle re-enactments o Christmas day.

*

After the death of Mum's parents, the Christmas dinner was held at ou family home. Mum would spend two weeks tidying the house, sho ping and cooking for the dinner, trying out recipes, making Christma cards and shopping for presents for the grandchildren. Dad's only tas was to pour the wine and carve the meat. He would invariably pick u the carving knife and fork, slice a piece of meat and declare, 'The mea is overcooked.' It could be undercooked. His contribution to the dinne conversation was to respond to questions about art.

After dinner, several of us cleared up and washed the dishes. On year I was standing alone washing the last of the dishes when I heard clearing of the throat. I looked up to see Dad standing in the doorwa

'You're too thin,' he said.

A surge of disgust arose from deep within me. No words woul come. I wanted to say, 'Look at you, an overweight, unfit, blotchy re faced man. What have you done to contribute to Christmas? You hav not done a thing.' He had *invited* my disgust.

Mum tells the story of a time early in their marriage.

'Ursula had come to dinner. Ursula and John were talking abou Thomas Mann's *The Magic Mountain*. I was listening to the conve sation when I heard a reference to Beethoven's Piano Sonata No. 3 Op. 111.

'"I know that piece," I said.

'Straight away John replied, "No, you don't. You wouldn't kno anything about Beethoven."

'"I'm sorry John," I said. "You're mistaken. I *do* know that piece o music."

'"Don't be ridiculous," he said. "What would you know?"

'"I do know that piece," I said. "I know that piece off by heart. I layed it in one of my music exams."

'John still did not believe me. Ursula believed me. John thought he ad married a silly little girl. He had no idea.'

Vhat would you know? You dope.'

'You fathead. Don't you know anything? Don't they teach you anyhing at school/university?'

I used to think Dad's remarks were about me or Mum or whichever ne of us he was addressing. He was the father, the man in authority. ow I know he was telling us about himself. He was telling us of his wn self-loathing.

I had imagined tipping my father out of the car, leaving him to ander lost on the country road. I want to express my anger at him or how he undermined us. I want T to get him to see how he inflicted is self-loathing onto his wife and children and the damage he had one in doing so. It is not likely that he would report to T on his underaining of his wife and children. T could *conclude* this is how he spoke o his children from how he speaks to him.

*

n the next session he says to T:

Anyway, I don't know why I am here. You're supposed to be helpng me but what would you know? You're only a psychotherapist or hatever. I don't even know what you are. Yes, I do know, you're a harlatan. You might think you know everything about me, but you on't. You don't know what I am not telling you. Ha ha ha. Who do ou think you are? All life is a series of defeats. Each parent aims to orrect the mistakes of their parents, but we never succeed. The artist orks out his despair in his painting. I doubt that Goya saw anyone called a 'psychotherapist'. What good would it have done him? I might not have painted those magnificent, troubling works. Heler father was a psychiatrist, but if *he* didn't have any luck with Stephe how could *you* have any luck with me? I don't know why I am he Man hands on misery to man, that is the human condition. There a no pills for melancholia, for existential angst, there are no words th would cure what deeply troubles us as human beings. You are n giving me an instruction manual, you hardly say a word, leaving r to do the talking. What use is that? What have you got to show for your work, whatever it is? You could hardly call it 'work', sitting or chair muttering a few words whenever you felt like it. At least an art has his painting. What do you have to show for yourself? Nothing.

T: You are wallowing in your sense of yourself as a defeated ma You are relishing your despair. You seem to think your misery giv you deeper insight into the human condition than those superfic idiots who are capable of joy. You are not aware of the depths of yo misogyny. None of us are. You nurture your self-loathing, dishing out to others, undermining your wife and children, if it's anything li what you say to me. You are constantly finding fault, criticising oth people's effort. You might be gifted with a certain sort of intelligen you might be talented at painting, you might have painted some ma nificent works, but ultimately you go to the grave like everybody els

He gets up and leaves before the end of the session.

I want him to claim his self-loathing, to divest myself of its shadow.

*

The next session he says:

I remember an incident in my first year of teaching at Melbour Grammar. A boy in the sixth form had refused to do what I asked I told him to stay back after the other boys had left. He was slouchi th disdain in this well-equipped art room, muttering, 'Art is stupid. 't is a waste of time. It doesn't lead anywhere. What use is art?' He ıs mouthing what I assumed were his parents' platitudes about art.

I grabbed the lapels of his expensive blazer with the embroidered otif and its Latin insignia. I dragged him towards the wall and banged s head against it. The sound of the head hitting the wall made me vare of the brutality I was inflicting on him. 'You don't realise how rtunate you are!' I said, hit hit hit against the wall. 'You are squan-ring your opportunities.' Hit hit. 'You know nothing. You know othing! You dill, you idiot.'

Here he was, in this most prestigious of private schools, telling me at art is a waste of time. My parents could not afford the uniform the minor private school which meant I could not take up the holarship. I had not even got to the sixth form. I had to leave school earn money.

I remember preparing my defence in the event that the boy reported e incident to his parents. His father may have been a lawyer, a bar-ster or a judge. As it happened, he gave me no further trouble. In fact, emember praising him for his *Still Life of Apples and Oranges in the anner of Cézanne.*

T: In telling me that you were unprofessional in banging the boy's ead against the wall in your frustration, you are telling me that I was ıprofessional in giving you my tirade, such as it was.

I am telling you that I am now prepared to do the work, whatever at is.

*

the next session, he says to T:

As I was walking down the street to come here, I felt a pang of ıxiety at the sight of the director of the National Gallery walking towards me. I feared he would ask me where I was going. As he cam closer, I realised it was someone else and then as I continued walking remembered Mother hitting me with my father's belt for playing wi the lower-class boys in the next street.

T: You felt ashamed of coming to see me. Your mother was asham of being lower class. She took out her resentment in hitting you wi your father's belt.

You fathead. You don't know anything.

T: If the way you speak to me is anything like the way you spo to your children, you were not literally hitting them, you were unde mining them with 'fatheads', 'dills', 'dopes'. As you did not know wh your mother hit you for playing with the lower-class boys, they wou not have known that you were speaking of your own self-loathing.

They will have to work that out for themselves.

*

In the next session he says:

You may have noticed that I didn't retaliate when you referred my self-loathing. It reassured me. It was as if you had always know and only then considered it the right time to tell me.

T: So we are getting somewhere. Congratulations.

I remember the first time I was asked to pretend to be someor I wasn't. I had given my first lecture on art. People in the audienc were putting up their hands asking questions expecting me to kno the answers as if I was some kind of expert. You appear to be someor who knows because of your position and yet you don't know. I felt lik an impostor. I remember thinking, Who do you think you are? Who d you think you are pretending you know when you don't?

The same thing happened in the army. I was barely twenty-fo years old when I became promoted above the other lads the same ag as me. The men came to me with their problems, feeling inadequat r the tasks demanded of them, missing their mothers, worried about hat they would do when they returned to civilian life. Some like me ere experiencing their first time away from home. They imagined lidn't have the problems they had because of my position.

T: Perhaps you imagine that I have everything worked out, I don't ave any problems. I am here totally for you.

Well, aren't you?

*

the next session he says:

I have not told you about the scholarship painting, a painting I ntered in the Travelling Scholarship prize. The scholarship was warded on the submission of a major painting in the final year of the t school. The winner was given an allowance to travel overseas for x months to study the paintings of the great masters. I was determined to win the prize. I was older than most of the other students. had read novels, philosophy and poetry. I had thought long and hard oout the role of the Australian artist after the war, concluding that ie artist must say something about the Australian identity but work ithin the tradition of the European masters. It was incumbent on the tist not to paint gum trees like Streeton and McCubbin, but to make comment on the suburban landscape.

With this understanding of the role of the artist, I embarked on painting of the beach at Mentone. I had studied Seurat's painting *Sunday Afternoon on the Island of La Grand Jatte* and applied the ame vision to the painting I would call *The Beach*.

I remember the elation at having solved the problems of the painting. I knew this would become a formative work in my career and that would develop what I had learnt in the subsequent work. Winning ie prize would launch my career as an artist and confirm that I had ade the right decision to be an artist. It would indicate to Mother that

I had talent. It would allow me to travel overseas to see Rembrandt painting *The Jewish Bride* which I had wanted to see in the origin ever since seeing a reproduction of it.

For six months after the winner was announced I found myse replaying the moment the name was called out. When one expects t hear one's own name and hears the name of another, one naturall thinks, 'There must be some mistake. They have got it all wron I didn't understand it. Without much effort I had always been nea the top of the class of sixty students. I had won the scholarship to th private school.

My despondency was relieved every so often with bouts of fur for Professor Joe Burke, the head of the judging panel. Apart fron Ursula Hoff, never again did I trust people at the university. Despit my distrust of the judges, I feared they were right. I feared that I wa deluding myself in thinking I had talent. I feared that I would be bette off doing something else. However, I knew deep within myself tha the judges were wrong, and I would prove them wrong eventually.

Helen's trite efforts at consolation only exacerbated my disa pointment. It suited her that I did not get the scholarship, not that sh would admit it. If I had won, I would have travelled overseas for si months, leaving her at home with the new baby, feeling resentment a not visiting the galleries herself. While I knew she was right—'it is jus a prize'—the depression overwhelmed me. I wanted to eradicate th experience to spite the judges and to spite myself.

'I might as well burn the wretched thing,' I said to Helen, as if burn ing the painting would destroy the evidence that it had ever existed.

'Don't you dare,' she replied as if I was threatening to cut off th electricity.

She saw the painting as partly hers. I realised then that she saw m career as also hers. We were in this together.

I know now that it wasn't that I had failed to win the scholarshi prize. It was that I had been convinced that I would win it. It was hubri

T: You have told me of your hubris after identifying your self-
)athing.

What have I got to lose?

remember what was referred to as 'the scholarship painting'. It's a each scene looking from the water towards the shore. A woman in athers is standing on the shoreline, protectively placing her hand on child's head. Her skin is pale to bright pink. A young, spindly man ; drying his hair with a striped towel; a woman in black is sitting in /hat seems like a reverie; a man in a hat and a suit is standing on the each, just looking. I wondered what he was doing there. He seemed ut of place.

Years later, I wondered if Dad had put himself in the painting as ne man just looking. Sometimes he would come into the room where I /as doing my homework. I would hear him clearing his throat. I would urn to see him. Then he would leave. I wondered if he wanted to say omething.

*

le says to T:

I will always remember my first exhibition opening at Peter Bray allery in 1956. After the hanging I walked through the rooms with he gallery director. The paintings looked more impressive with the ghting in the gallery than when balanced against the wall in the tudio. However, I could not help comparing the work to Cézanne and 'icasso, aware that it failed to live up to their accomplishments. Then I hought, 'This is not Paris 1910, this is Melbourne, Australia, 1956.' had no doubt that I was making a serious comment, establishing an lentity and a purpose for Australian art.

T: You could allow yourself to be impressed.

When Helen Ogilvie, the gallery director, pronounced her verdi 'Simply marvellous,' I realised that the next time I would stand in th room, friends, relatives, artists and critics would be looking at wha had spent a year working on in the little shed in the backyard. Th may not be thinking 'simply marvellous' or even 'a little bit marv lous'. I remember thinking, 'What if the critics failed to see what I w doing?'

On the tram going home after the hanging of the exhibition glanced at my fellow travellers sullenly reading their newspape I remember thinking how much easier to have a job in an office. Th with no warning, Mother's words spoke from within me, 'Now lo what you've done.' Although she had not been invited to the exhi tion, I wanted her to see the paintings, to be proud of what I had do I wanted her to see that I was a serious artist.

T: You wanted to return to that time when you had the power make your mother smile, to make her proud of your accomplishmen to receive her applause.

Mother's 'now look what you've done' spoke to me as if the bott of milk had slipped from my hands, not as the achievement of havi an exhibition of paintings, my inaugural exhibition.

In *The Silent Woman*, Janet Malcolm writes, 'Art is theft, art is arm robbery, art is not pleasing your mother.' If this thought appeal to me, it would surely appeal to my father. I want to give him th quote but when speaking to T he says what comes into his head that moment. I doubt that Janet Malcolm wrote this sentence just as came into her head. A lot of thought went into crafting that sentenc

He says to T:

In my attempt to obliterate Mother's voice from within me, I can up with a private manifesto: Art is freeing oneself from one's mothe ambitions. Art is not seeking applause from one's mother…

T: ...and art is not seeking the applause from whoever stands in the ace of one's mother.

hen Dad sold only one or two paintings at an exhibition, he would ılk around the house gloomily muttering, 'I refuse to paint pretty ctures of flowers.'

*

the next session he says:

I had grievances towards Mother. Helen's mother had grievances wards me for marrying her daughter. I remember the moment she emed to accept me.

One Sunday morning about 4 am I was woken by Helen's tossing d churning accompanied by muffled cries of pain. She was seven onths pregnant. I feared something was happening to the baby, but e would not let me ring the doctor, assuring me that she would be right. I felt utterly helpless. In my ineptitude, I fetched a couple of pros and a glass of water. The writhing and the muffled moaning ntinued for about an hour as I attempted to doze off to sleep. I did t know what to do when Helen became more and more flustered, cking off the sheets and blankets as if the pain had possessed her. en, after a silence, she let out a piercing scream. Something slithery d spilled from between her legs. It was bluish, streaked with blood d hardly bigger than my hand. I could barely recognise it for what was. I remember thinking, 'This is not meant to be happening, this is t meant to be happening.'

I fumbled in Helen's handbag, searching for the doctor's phone ımber and then I heard a cry. The baby was alive.

The doctor arrived, cut the umbilical cord and wrapped the baby in shawl. Despite the reassurance of his presence, my heart continued unding. I got dressed. A taxi had been called to take Helen to the hospital. I was aware that something practical was demanded of m so I scooped up the bloodstained sheets and got in the taxi with Hel and the baby, asking Helen helplessly what I should do with the bloo stained sheets.

When we arrived at the hospital, Helen was whisked away wi the baby, leaving me in the taxi without her. It was nearly 8 am as walked up the garden path of her mother's house. I knocked on th front door and as soon as it opened I thrust the bloodied sheets in Helen's mother's arms.

'Helen had her baby,' I said, handing the evidence. I was led in the dining room where she left me to take the sheets to the laund I helped myself to some cold toast and fumblingly spread it wi strawberry jam as I tried to stop myself from bursting into tears. Th enormity of what had happened was beginning to become clear Helen had given birth to her baby. When Helen's mother returned sh referred to me as 'dear' and I knew then that I had been accepted.

That afternoon I went to the hospital to see Helen who was sittir up in bed. The baby was born two months premature and weighe only three pounds. The doctor told us that she was not likely live. Two months later Helen went to the hospital and brought th baby home.

T: I'm astonished. It must have been traumatic for Helen and als for you.

I had never considered it traumatic. You have to realise that Hele is a stoic. The worst thing was my incompetence. I had no idea wh to do. I felt utterly helpless. I knew nothing about childbirth. Fathe were not permitted at the birth.

T: What stopped you from ringing the doctor?

Helen didn't want me to interrupt the important man at 4 am on Sunday morning.

T: And what about the two months when you didn't know if th baby would live?

I took Helen's expressed milk into the hospital on the way to work. ne day I felt a wet patch on my legs and realised that the glass bottle as leaking. Fearing that the baby would die, I alighted at the next ation and took a taxi to the hospital, leaving me with no money for y lunch. I explained to the nurse that the bottle was leaking, fear- g that too much milk would be lost. It seemed that Helen had been kpressing more milk than the baby could take in and the leftover milk as being fed to babies whose mothers did not have sufficient.

'hen I was eleven years old, Mum took me to visit a nurse who had orked at the hospital. As the nurse appeared from behind the flywire oor of her home, Mum pointed at me and said, 'See, she didn't die.'

Eighteen months after my birth, Vicky was born; eighteen months ter Freda was born, and then Charlotte. Four children in less than x years.

*

e tells T:

After the birth of our first and second child, I was very busy paint- g, determined to establish myself as an artist. I would have been appy to ignore Mother. The children had one grandmother; I didn't e why they needed another. Somehow Helen got it into her head that grandmother should see her grandchildren. She was naïvely oblivi- us of Mother's hostility towards her, but as far as I was concerned, if e wanted to see Mother that was her business.

It did not surprise me when a rift opened up between them. Mother ad given the children lollies and said, 'Don't tell Mummy.' Naturally e children did tell Mummy. 'She is teaching the children to tell lies,' elen complained. 'She is teaching the children to keep secrets from eir mother.' Mother would see the lollies as a way of endearing her- elf to her grandchildren. She would see it as her prerogative to spoil her grandchildren, but Helen expected me to tell Mother not to do thi again. To appease her, I wrote a brief note as she had asked.

T: You wrote the note knowing it would antagonise your mother.

If this rupture between Helen and Mother had not happened the sooner or later something else would have caused it.

Two weeks after Freda was born, Helen told me she intended visi ing Mother with the new baby. I advised her not to go. That evenin she reported on the visit.

'Mr Brack opened the door and said, "I'll get Mother" and whe Mrs Brack came to the door, she shouted at me to go away, screamin at me.'

'Serves you right,' I said. 'I told you not to go.'

T: That must have been very distressing for Helen. Very distressin to be turned away with the new baby and then told 'serves you right

I told her not to go and she ignored my advice. What did she expect

T: You were unsympathetic.

It justified severing my relationship with Mother. There was n announcement, no ceremonial cutting of a ribbon. Mother did not ge in touch with me until ten years later when she rang to speak to me o the phone.

I wondered what would propel a grandmother to turn away her daugh ter-in-law holding a new baby, a two-year-old and a three-year-old b her side, having travelled on public transport to get there. The anger a her daughter-in-law must have been insurmountable.

I cannot remember Dad's mother giving me the lollies saying, 'Don tell Mummy.' I can remember washing my hands in her bathroor basin. The soap was like a golden jewel, translucent brown. It wasn opaque green like the soap we had at home.

Dad painted a picture called *Mother and Son*. He doesn't call it 'm mother' but given what I know about his relationship with his mothe it seems to me that it could be no one else.

:e tells T:

After I had cut myself off from Mother, bouts of anger at her would emind me that she still had the power to upset me. I wanted to do omething with this anger once and for all so I did the only thing I new: I embarked on a painting called *Mother and Son*. Mother would ot see it for the very reason that she had no interest in my paintings.

I remember painting the mother's face, pinched in, disapproving, avenously scowling. The eyes squint through framed spectacles, taring into the distance. The son stands behind his mother, a helmet f thick hair carefully brushed, his collar neatly done up, his mouth urned up in the faintest hint of a smile. The son bursts with promise, efusing to be cowed by his mother's disapproval. One wonders how his shrivelled woman could have produced this statuesque young ıan glowing with the potential of all life ahead of him.

I had originally painted the mother and son against a drab grey-lue sky but then recalling Mother's comment that an artist merely abbled', I found myself dabbling a pattern of white clouds, thinking, will show you dabbling.' When I looked at it in reproduction several ears later, I realised that the clouds were a caricature of clouds like a hild would draw to fill in the background. They were thought balloons, mpty with nothing to say. Nothing to say between the mother and ıe son.

T: The thought balloons say nothing but, as you describe it, the icture says a lot.

I regretted selling the painting. I had not expected it would sell. If it ad not been sold, I would have burnt it. It was a shameful documen-ary of my thoughts about Mother, not that anyone would see it as ıy' mother. Mother did the best that she could. I don't blame her for vanting better things for her sons. I wanted better things for myself.

am trying to remember my grandmother. Dad was trying to forget er. Severing a relationship with a parent does not cut them out of one's existence. The parent comes to us in dreams. The parent lives our unconscious. The sculptor Henry Moore remembers rubbing h mother's back with liniment when he came home from school. S suffered terribly from rheumatism. Years later, in making the scu ture of a seated figure of a woman, he found himself 'unconsciou giving to its back the long-forgotten shape of the one I had so oft rubbed as a boy.'

*

T: You wanted better things for yourself. Your mother wanted bett things for you. What about your father?

There's an image of my father that has stayed with me from chi hood. I had got up very early to go to the outside lavatory. On the w back I caught sight of my father wheeling his bike coming home fro night shift. 'So this is what work is,' I thought. It explained Mothe eagerness that we not have a job like our father. It wasn't just t expression on my father's face, it is what happened after. When saw me, his face transformed, and I knew then that he concealed h dejection from me.

If I was disheartened by the work in the insurance office, shift wo in the brewery would be even more disheartening. Office work w 9 am to 5 pm. I was sitting at a desk adding up figures. After masteri what was required of me an onerous, dreary boredom set in. I shou have felt ecstatic leaving work at the end of the day, but boredom h destroyed any capacity for rejoicing. I remember walking along t street thinking that I should not be feeling like this in a job so mu 'better' than my father's. If it were not for the Hill of Content booksh and enrolling in the night class at the gallery school, I do not kn what would have become of me.

After returning from the army I found myself once again in the ci at 5 pm, waiting for Stephens in the doorway of his office in Colli reet. We were having a drink after work. As I waited, I was struck the uniformly grim expressions on the faces of the office workers alking to the railway station. Despite leaving work to make their way me, the dejection of the work had fixed itself on their faces. The ought came to me, 'I could put this into a painting.'

These people who worked in offices in the day retreated to the burbs in the night. They appeared to be haunted by existential gst, an unidentified ennui which was more than the boredom of e job. I stood in the doorway sketching the figures walking down the reet, striving to capture their facial expressions, their clothes, their annerisms. I had planned on painting an anonymous crowd in the stance, but given that the impersonal crowd is a cliché, close up ere would have to be individual portraits, otherwise the painting ould fail through facile overstatement. It struck me as almost eerie be sketching within three feet of so many people, none of whom ok the slightest notice of me. Although the faces in my painting ere based on actual people, I altered them to represent generic types, inting the recognisable face of John Stephens and Helen's father ho worked in Collins Street.

All portraits are, at some level, a reflection of the artist. I was aware at in painting the figures walking down the street I was investing ch with the same lack of enchantment that I had experienced work-g in the office.

T: You are telling me that *Collins St 5pm* had its genesis in your emory of walking down the street in your first job working in an fice. Perhaps it has its genesis further back in the memory of your ther returning home from shift work. If that is so, the person who d 'inspired' the painting was of necessity absent from it. Your ther was not walking home from work at 5 pm carrying a briefcase earing a jacket and a tie. He was coming home in the early hours of e morning, his clothes tainted with the smell of the factory where worked.

I want my father to make some reference to his father. I want to belie that his father's work had some bearing on his own.

He continues with what he has previously said in interview:

It was arrogant of me to see the workers like this. The painti appeared to be saying, 'Look at those pathetic little people with the boredom and their dull lives. I am different from them. I am an arti At the art school we considered ourselves superior to the office work the factory worker, the tradesman. We might be poor, but we had vocation, we were not working for a boss. I should have known th the lives of the office workers were as complex as mine, if not mo In the arrogance of youth, I had no respect for the lives of my paren I just wanted to get away from them. I wanted to get away from t poverty and dismalness of my childhood.

Through no fault of my own *Collins St 5pm* became a famo Australian painting. You would think that an artist would be pleas that his work had become so well known, but it means that one permanently identified with that work. The irony is that the work th creates a sense of identity and belonging was painted by a man wh felt that he never belonged.

T: Perhaps none of us feel we belong. Perhaps that is our belongi

*

In 1953, two years before Dad painted *Collins Street 5pm*, he paint *The New House*, a painting of a man and a woman standing togeth in a living room. The man has one hand in the pocket of his suit jack the other around the woman's waist, clasping her like a doll. One of t woman's hands rests lightly near his tie while her head nestles on h shoulder. The man is in profile, sternly cold. The woman looks direct at us, smiling. The man is wearing a suit, the woman wears a dre a frilled apron around her waist. The painting appears to be sayi ɔok at these people proudly standing in their new house. They think ɩe new house will make them happy. I know better.'

I wondered about the house in which Dad was raised.

e says to T:

I remember one of the last times I saw Mother. I had visited her ◦ collect my birth certificate. I was annoyed with her frustration ◦ssicking in the kitchen cupboard drawer, so I removed myself to the ʼont room, a room reserved for visitors which I was now qualified to ɩter. In Mother's absence my eyes did a circuit of the room, noticing ɩe couch, the chairs, the wireless, the little figurines imprisoned in a ass cabinet. There was not a single book and not a single picture on ɩe wall and although the room was cleaned and dusted as a showcase ◦r visitors, to my knowledge few visitors ever came.

Mother found the birth certificate, which she thrust into my hands— ; if in handing over the record of my birth she was relinquishing the ɔn whose birth it recorded. Later, when I looked at the two signatures ɑder my name, I wondered how it was that I had been born from these vo people who were so different from me in every way imaginable.

T: They may have been wondering the same thing themselves.

I imagined I had successfully extricated myself from Mother and ʼom Pater. They had occasionally come to me in dreams. Never before nce talking to you have they returned night after night. *You* have ɩade them return. You have surreptitiously laid out the red carpet ◦r them.

T: Our parents live on in our unconscious. It is what we are working ɑ here. It is the material we work with.

ŀy unconscious takes me to Kafka's letter to his father.

'Dearest Father, You asked me recently why I maintain that I am fraid of you. As usual, I was unable to think of any answer to your uestion, partly for the very reason that I am afraid of you...'

Kafka never sent the forty-seven-page letter to his father, an since the executor of his will did not burn all his writings as instructe the letter Kafka's father never read can now be read by anyone wh searches on the internet.

Kafka wrote, 'A book can be the axe for the frozen sea within u There is no point in a book that does not wake us up, disturb us.'

I give these words to my father.

He tells T:

The artist works with the unconscious. The painting is wide ope to interpretation, its meaning is inexhaustible. A painting can be th axe for the frozen sea within us. There is no point in a painting tha does not wake us up, disturb us.

T: Are you telling me that there is no point to being here if it doe not wake you up, disturb you? Are you telling me that you are pr pared to be disturbed, to break the frozen sea inside you?

I refused to paint pretty pictures of flowers.

*

In the next session he says to T:

I see you have a vase of poppies in your room. In my paintin *The Bar*, I put a vase of poppies on the bar.

The Bar was inspired by one of the great paintings of the nin teenth century, Manet's *A Bar at the Folies-Bergère*. I was struck b the observation that the life it reflects so vividly and sensuously n longer exists. It seemed like a good idea, almost a century later, to d another painting of the bar, a painting of a life that does exist.

I painted it in 1954 when pubs closed at 6 pm. Now *that* life n longer exists. In Manet's painting, a barmaid stands in front of mirror reflecting the other side of the bar. My barmaid also stands i front of a mirror. The bar in my painting is a synthesis of several bar nd although the barmaid is a portrait, she was actually an attendant 1 a milkbar, a woman who seemed to fit better with my conception f a barmaid. Years later, I realised that in her regal domination of 1e small space, her hand firmly on the cloth, the barmaid bears an ncanny resemblance to Helen.

omeone once asked the poet Les Murray if he was a tall poppy. 'No, am a gorgeous spreading hydrangea,' he said.

[e says to T:

Most bars have no flowers at all. The vase of Iceland poppies ymbolised the suburbia of the 1950s. These were the sort of bought owers people had in vases. Someone once asked if I was a tall poppy. Jo,' I said, 'I am the host of golden daffodils I saw wandering lonely as child.'

*

read somewhere that, 'John Brack sees the twentieth century in a tate of precarious balance.'

In the next session, he says to T:

Every so often I return to that moment when I literally fell into the utter. I remember thinking, 'This is the still point of the turning world.' he actual fall was a blessed relief from the increasing dread that I vould succumb to dementia. I lived in terror that I would end up like ıy friend Perceval who needed a minder and could no longer paint as e once did. All my life I have lived with a sense of ominousness as if ıings were in a state of precarious balance, things about to fall.

I was born in 1920, two years after the end of the First World War. was nineteen at the beginning of the Second World War. In that ɔrmative time of my life between the wars it is understandable that 'sensitive' child would pick up a premonition of uncertainty from the headlines in the newspaper, the news on the radio, talk about impending war after the war that was meant to end all wars. I oft feared that a tower of blocks would topple over within me. I fear that I would fall into the abyss of oblivion. Painting did somethi with this sense of things about to fall. The act of painting was li stamping one's foot on a piece of paper to stop it from flying aw in the wind. The control over the paintbrush gave me the illusion holding things still, of holding myself from falling.

This sense of precariousness drew me to find the subject of r paintings in the form of jockeys, gymnasts and ballroom dance poised in precarious balance almost to the point of slipping or falli over. Everyday items were positioned in a state of falling—knives a forks, pens and pencils. Floorboards and Persian carpets were plac at disconcerting angles, suggestive of falling. I knew that if it were n for painting, I myself would feel as if I was toppling into the abyss.

My father's sense of things about to fall may have been exacerbat by what I saw as the self-medication to relieve it. I remember ironi my school dress in the kitchen when Dad would come in wearing h dressing gown. He would say nothing. He would pour himself a gla of water, drop the Alka-Seltzer tablet into the water, watch it fizz u and as I moved the iron back and forth over the blue, yellow and whi checks, I would glance at the fizzing water, aware of Dad waiting f the tablet to be completely dissolved and then gulping. I knew t Alka-Seltzer was for the hangover from the previous night's drinki which was an attempt to take the edge off the depression.

Depression inhabits the house. It asks to be respected. One fea that if it is not respected, it will do more than fizz up and dissol it will obliterate the bearer of it and consequently the whole fami I often sensed that at any moment someone could pull an imagina tablecloth off our kitchen table and everything on the surface wou fall—plates, knives, forks and spoons. It was not only the twentie ntury that was in a state of precarious balance. It was our own ree-bedroom weatherboard home in the suburb of Surrey Hills.

: says to T:

Sometimes in the morning the precariousness would strike in at moment between waking up and starting on the day. Drinking leviated the sense of things about to fall. Fortunately, my muscle emory kept me painting, and I never failed to come up with ideas for inting, even if they were variations on a theme. Ultimately, I main-ined the discipline required of an artist helped along by the ordered, edictable routine of family life. Once or twice the break in routine hen Helen was in hospital sent me into a state of anxiety, added to e fact that I was required to do something about the dinner and the usehold chores.

Thankfully these visits to you are the same time every day. I am amed within the fifty-minute session.

*

hen you live with a painting, you come to see things in it you didn't e at first sighting. If the artist is your father you cannot see the inting separately from your experience of him as a father.

Dad's painting *The Scissors Shop* hung in the house I lived in hen I left home. Three rows of surgical scissors are opened and shut shades of black, dark aqua, blue-green. They are placed on three elves against a lurid pink background suggestive of opened flesh. 1 the top of the cabinet two hands are spread out, palms facing ownward onto the glass. The hands are those of Dad's friend Hal attam, a gynaecologist who collected paintings. Once, when he was ving Dad a lift in his car, the glove box sprung open and his surgical issors tumbled out.

I lived with the painting *The Scissors Shop*. I saw it subliminal Sometimes I stood and looked at it without distraction. Sometimes pictured the hands on the top of the cabinet picking up the scisso and cutting into open flesh.

Dad didn't just *draw* pictures of knives and scissors, he used the I remember looking through his bookshelves, taking out Céline's *Dea on The Instalment Plan*. I opened it up. A Stanley knife had been use to cut a small rectangle from within the pages of the book. Inside th cavern made by the cutting lay a bank book in Dad's name.

The menace was in the threat. The premonition that things wou fall. Dad walked up and down the hallway clenching his fists. H restrained his anger in the house, but his silence radiated aggressic Once, as Mum and I cleared up after lunch, he returned after leavir for the studio, said something provocative and then left before w could reply.

'He needs to do that,' Mum said. 'He needs to stir up some ang before he gets back to painting.'

*

Dad died in February 1999. A few years after his death, a retrospecti exhibition of his work was held at the National Gallery of Victor Almost all his paintings were displayed in the exhibition. He wa 'speaking' to us in his paintings. He was also speaking to us in grey fo printed directly onto the wall: 'What I paint most is what interests m most, that is, people; the human condition.'

A pang of anger hit me as I read those words. I wanted to say, 'Yc might have painted pictures of your four daughters but what wou you know of the human condition of any one of us?'

Competing voices arose from within me.

'How lucky you are to have those pictures of you.'

'That *Collins Street 5pm* is a masterpiece.'

'But what help was he when I fell off my bike and Mum wasn't ome?'

'What did he say when I was eight and didn't know who fought ho in the Second World War? "You dill."'

'Look at how marvellous the paintings of the pencils and pens, how naginative, how ingenious.'

'Where were you when we were on holiday at the beach?'

'We are so lucky to have those etchings of the four of us.'

'Remember the gloom when paintings didn't sell…'

'But look at the brilliance of those portraits and the nudes on ne Persian rugs.'

'And where were you when one of us was ill?'

'Those pictures of the postcards are superb: the colours, the raftsmanship…'

'Where was your support for Mum?'

'But look at those portraits of Mum when she was younger; she ooks severe in the later portrait, but also regal and self-possessed.'

'How lucky to see the inner life of your father in the paintings, ne lifetime's work. It's a mighty achievement.'

Vhat I paint most is what interests me most, that is, people; the human ondition.'

You rarely showed much 'interest' in us. We are people. We are uman.

I wanted to say to my father, 'It's not just that you didn't show nuch interest in us; it is the grandiosity of "the human condition". Vhat gives you the entitlement to speak on behalf of others, the mnipotence to know something about all humans from your own mited experience?' The audacity of it. Mum would never claim to peak of the human condition.

An uneasiness arose as I became alert to other writers and artist referring to 'the human condition'. In reconsidering my resistance to I remembered listening to Mum's recording of the American comedia Ruth Draper. As a society hostess she gives a monologue translatin Dante for her Italian lesson. She concludes with her translation:

'Midway in the journey of my life
I found myself in a dark forest
because the direct way was lost.'

How could one 'find oneself' in the dark forest? I wondered. If yo were sensible, wouldn't you see yourself going into the forest? And you saw yourself going in, wouldn't you find your way out?

Yet I knew from my own adolescence that I had not *decided* to as the questions, 'Who am I? Where do I belong? What is my purpose i life?' The questions had arisen from within. I had *found myself* askin those questions midway between childhood and adulthood.

Isn't this 'the human condition'? We *find* ourselves lost in the dar forest, not having known how we arrived there, seeking to find way out?

Now I understood it. My own idiosyncratic wonderings wer not particular to me but an aspect of being human. If we keep ou thoughts and feelings private, we have no way of knowing that other share the same troubles and worries that we do.

*

He tells T:

I remember when I knew that I was not alone in the world, not freakish isolate, that my anguish was an aspect of being human. I wa fifteen when I read a short story. Two adolescent boys meet on th beach where their families are staying for the summer holidays. A they swim, dabble in rock pools and laze in the sun, they talk abou ıeir worries about what they are going to be when they grow up. ach of the boys does not want to be what their father wants them › be and yet, in choosing what they want to do, they fear their ıther's disappointment. One of the boys does not want to enter the ımily business. He wants to be an actor. The other wants to write. .t the end of the holidays, they return to their homes in different ›wns, each feeling the loss of the friendship they have made over the ummer holiday.

My parents could not afford a summer holiday at the beach. I did ot have a friend, but I knew then that other boys had the same ques- .ons as I did, questions that I had never articulated to myself. This ; what adolescence is, I thought, this worry about finding what one ⁄ants to do in life, not what one's parents want for us. This is universal.

T: As an adolescent you were reassured at not being alone.

And then as an adult I read André Malraux's novel *La Condition Iumaine* and Hannah Arendt's philosophical treatise *The Human Con- ition.* Magritte named a painting *La Condition Humaine*. The titles npressed me. Through our understanding of the human condition ⁄e connect through literature and art. This was my thinking when an ıterviewer asked, 'How do you choose what to paint?' I found myself esponding: 'What I paint most is what interests me most, that is, eople; the human condition. The artist's motive is to understand and › illuminate for others.'

When the interview was written up in the newspaper, my refer- nce to 'the human condition' was used as a headline for the interview.

Helen would not let it go. 'The arrogance of it. I mean, I ask you! Vho do you think you are? The human condition.'

T: Perhaps that is what we are doing here, exploring 'the human ondition'.

*

When tidying up for visitors, we could never find a place for a sing snakeskin shoe with a silver buckle. The leather lining was emboss with the name of a shop in London, written in gold cursive scri Without any designated purpose, it sat on a mantelpiece, a booksh a toy box: an emblem of my mother's childhood.

There was not a single remnant from my father's childhood, photograph, nothing.

He says to T:

You want me to say whatever comes into my mind. Nothing com to mind. Nothing. My mind has gone blank. I once painted a portr of Kim Bonython who was known as an art collector, racing car id tity, jazz enthusiast, bon vivant. After the portrait was completed received a letter from him asking if in 'that blank area in the top rig hand corner of the picture' I could paint his celebrated chequer cap. I wrote back saying, 'There is no blank area in the top right-ha corner of the picture' but that if he liked I would paint a separa painting of his treasured cap. As an art collector you would think th he would know that the blank in the painting is saying something.

T: The blank in the painting is saying something as the silence this room is saying something.

The blank in the painting is nothing like the blank of the canv before one starts a painting. Every time one faces the blank canv one is struck with terror. You would think it would diminish over t years, but it never does. To alleviate the terror, I always started a ne picture before finishing the last.

T: What was your first experience of terror?

I was ten years old. Mother was one of nine children. We we visiting one of her sisters who lived in the country. I had never be to the country before. After lunch Mother and Aunty Ivy did t washing up while the rest of us set out on a little path weaving i way through the gum trees. Lindsay and I took up the rear walki

silence, deep in our own thoughts. The only sounds were the twit-
ring of birds and the occasional twig snapping underfoot. I stopped take a stone out of my shoe and then continued on the path, while ndsay walked ahead. The thought came to me, 'I am all alone in this orld.' The silence was broken by the piercing cry of a bird soaring erhead, a shrill cry echoing through the landscape as if the cry was lling from inside me. I was hit with the terror of the question, 'Who n I? What am I doing in this world?' The question struck me like the ercing of an arrow.

The echo of the cry persisted until I came upon the others peering to an empty well. My father picked up a stone and dropped it into e well. A few seconds later the echo announced that it had reached destination. A dread came into my stomach as if I myself had been opped into the well. I picked up a stone and dropped it in and then cked up another and another. I was aware of Lindsay speaking to me, it I felt cut off from him and everybody else.

When we arrived home, my father paused before going in the front oor, remarking to all of us and no one in particular, 'It's nice to have e concrete under the feet.'

Later that night I recalled the terror. I assumed it was particular to e but then I wondered if my father had also experienced the terror, iowing that it was not something one could speak about to another, ast of all one's father.

T: You wondered about having a rapport with your own father as u had with Helen's father.

In 1947, at the age of twenty-seven, I painted a picture of a boy nning, his eyes bulging in terror, his mouth wide open in a silent ream. I called it *Little Boy Lost,* an expression of that romantic eling characteristic of young people, saying, 'I am unhappy, lost to yself.' Now I see it as self-indulgent and naïve.

T: Your cynicism protects you.

Nothing protected me from the terror. Every so often an injectio of terror reinserted itself, accompanied by the anxiety of the thoug 'Who am I? What should I be doing with my life?' The discovery tha wanted to be an artist initially relieved me of the terror, but it return when I was not painting and invariably resurfaced when faced wi the blank canvas.

T: Do you feel the terror now?

No, I don't. I am at the still point of the turning world.

*

When I was fifteen, Mum took me to see Barry Humphries performi in his one-man show as Mrs Everage. As Mum says, 'In those da nobody had seen a man dressed up as a woman. That is what made terribly funny.' Over the years Mrs Everage became more outspok more daring, playing to larger audiences in mainstream theatres, n the little hall where I had first seen her. Elevated to 'Dame Edna', sh wore a wig, ornate spectacles and garishly beaded costumes, not th hat, simple frock and handbag of the housewife from Moonee Ponds

I do not know Dad's thoughts on Mrs Everage, but I do know wh he said in interview about painting a portrait of her.

He tells T:

When I first saw Barry Humphries as Mrs Everage, I recognis myself—another man feeling antipathy towards his mother. Barry too up dressing as the suburban housewife that his mother was, satirical mocking her in public on stage, flaunting his disregard for his moth Compared to Barry's mother, Mother had nothing to complain about

When Mrs Everage had become a cultural icon, I was asked to pai a portrait of Barry Humphries in the role of Mrs Everage.

The struggle with the painting felt insurmountable. I had nev painted a portrait of one person posing as another. When I muttere his is terrible, this is disastrous,' Barry kindly suggested giving up ıt I assured him that my mutterings were my highest form of praise. wasn't just that it was the portrait of one person posing as another. s the sittings progressed, my rapport with Barry fuelled my disdain r my own mother. Barry's mocking of his mother gave me permis-on to unleash on my own and I found myself having to resist the ɔmbined force of what we recognised in each other. We were like two ɔys egging each other on, pulling the wings off flies.

As Barry stepped out of the dress he wore as Mrs Everage, the ought came to me: 'One cannot easily step out of the influence of ıe's mother.' Here was Barry, more obviously than me, getting back his mother, making an art form of it. The grotesqueness of it both tracted and repulsed me.

When I looked at the finished painting and saw Mrs Everage look-g at me from the canvas—her large, gloved hands splayed over the ɔuch, her eyes leering at me—I realised I was looking at a vulture.

T: A vulture.

It was not only our mothers that Barry and I had in common. We ɔth took solace for what troubled us in drink. When Barry arrived my studio at 10 am for the sitting, he brought with him not only ıe costume, the wig, the powder and the lipstick, but a bottle of that ıastly tasting Italian drink, Fernet Branca.

'What's wrong with beer or wine?' I asked him.

'This is thirty-five percent alcohol,' he said.

I refused his offer of a swig, saying, 'It would be an offence to Mrs verage to be drinking on the job.'

A year or so after finishing the portrait, I heard that Barry was ɔund bashed lying in a carpark outside a pub after a heavy bout of rinking. He was taken to a private hospital to dry out. It rattled me hen I heard the news, not only for Barry's sake but for my own. told myself that it would not happen to me, as I was not drinking thirty-five percent alcohol at ten o'clock in the morning. Instead (taking what happened to Barry as a warning, I ignored it. When was found in the gutter drunk and sent to hospital to dry out, I had t confront not only the humiliation, but my own hubris.

T: *And now you are here.*

And now I am here. Were it not for falling in the gutter, I woul have lost my mind. I remember the fear when the paintbrush firs slipped from my hand. I knew it was a sign of something ominous.

T: What did you do with that fear?

I poured myself a drink.

*

The next session he says to T:

The memory of the paintbrush falling from my hand takes me t the first night home from the army when something bigger than paintbrush fell from me—the hope that Mother would approve of m decision to be an artist.

A few years later I remember looking at a reproduction of Rer brandt's *The Return of the Prodigal Son*. The Bible parable tells us tha the prodigal son returns, asking for forgiveness for having squandere his inheritance. I had done nothing to warrant my parents' forgiv ness. I was anything but prodigal. I was the eldest son who had t leave school to contribute to the finances of the family because m father was too poor to keep me at school. I had brought money int the family, not squandered it. I was the son who had ensured that hi younger brother stayed at school, not that I begrudged Lindsay thi opportunity. After studying Rembrandt's painting *The Return of th Prodigal Son* I embarked on a version of my own.

The Bible parable makes no reference to the mother. My paintin gives prominence to the mother. I remember painting the smirk on he ace. I remember taking a ruler to flatten her chest as if she had never ursed a child. In my painting the father sits blankly, resigned. The on sits between his mother and his father, looking at his plate down-ast, dispirited. The son appears to be going through the motions of ating his meal as if obediently doing what he is told. The son's hand poised on the knife in the act of eating his dinner. The mother's and is forcefully grasping a knife but with no dinner in front of her, here is no apparent purpose to the knife. The brother hovers in the oorway.

T: The painting is a message, a private declaration of your experi-nce of returning home after your time in the army.

It is a message to myself. My parents would never see the painting, ot having sufficient interest to come to the exhibition where it was hown. Stephens bought the painting. He knew the meaning of it. I ad no reason to give the painting any further thought until I was sked to look at the quality of the reproduction for a book. This time saw what I had not seen when focused on solving the problem of he painting. I saw the father, corpse-like, grim, scowling. I saw the isheartened son obediently poised over his frugal dinner. I saw he mother in her butcher's apron, clenching a knife in her fist, a mirk on her face. Then I saw what I had not seen before. I saw the rospect of the mother's hand rising and striking down the knife in a esture of castration.

T: You saw what you feared of your mother.

*

n the next session he says:

Early in our marriage, Helen was sitting on the couch reading *The Brothers Karamazov*, turning the pages and chuckling to herself. 'It's ot a comic book,' I said. She was only laughing, she said, 'because ow I know where you get your ideas from.'

Helen had accused me of getting my ideas from Dostoevsky b where did she get her ideas? She got them from me, of course. She w only reading *The Brothers Karamazov* because I had suggested th she did. You have to remember that she was barely twenty-one wh we first met. I was twenty-seven. In the beginning she got her ide from me but over the years it seemed that she got more and more ide of her own.

We had gone to dinner at Mac and Jessie's house. Gordon and Ka were also present. After dinner the women went into the kitchen wh Mac, Gordon and I adjourned to the sitting room where we discuss the problem of romanticism in poetry. When Mac left to fetch anoth bottle of wine, the thought came to me: none of our fathers wou have engaged in a conversation about literature. We were ambitio clever boys from the working class who had received a grant to ha an education. We had come far from our working-class beginnings.

When Mac returned, he reported that the women had finish the washing up and suggested that we invite them to come in a listen in to our conversation. As the wives sat down where M indicated they were to sit, I began to have doubts about the wisdo of this invitation. We continued our discussion where we had le off, but the ambiance had changed and I was aware that we we performing for an audience. Not only that, Helen and Kate found way of inserting themselves into the discussion, offering their ov ill-formed opinions.

We had barely driven off in the taxi when Helen remarked on ho 'ridiculous' we looked. She accused me of 'pomposity', of 'showi off', of 'competing' with Gordon and Mac. Instead of listening and learning something from us as Mac had envisaged, Helen ha launched into ridicule. 'We were *allowed* to listen in to your conv sation,' she said.

Helen was right. We *were* competing and showing off, but it was t way that she said it. She said it with contempt. I should have trust y instinct. I knew that it was a mistake to invite the women in. ac wanted to impress them. We were impressed with ourselves. We d sought each other out. Our wives were middle class. They were t thinking, 'Look how far we've come.'

T: You saw yourselves as 'lower' because of your class. You saw the omen as 'lower' because they were women, despite the fact that they ere middle class.

the next session he says to T:

Helen had been brought up in the genteel upper class where she arnt to talk to people, introduce people, shake hands. I had been ought up in a house of very few visitors with few social outings. elen had insisted I come to her parents' house for Christmas but it as Rudy who insisted I make the aeroplane flight to Sydney to meet llectors who were considering buying a painting. I loathed these ents which took a whole day away from painting.

From the moment we arrived, I found myself counting the minutes ntil it was time to go home. In my resentment at having to be there I ould hear Helen's declaration: 'I have never tasted anything so delious in my whole life.' I then recalled her hovering over the kitchen ble, dipping her spoon into the saucepan, scraping the remains as her nner. I would observe her nodding at the man next to her, laughing, casionally saying a few words and then on the plane going home e would tell me, 'such an odious little man' and accuse me of sitting ere glumly looking at my watch.

T: You are telling me how much work Helen put into your career.

That was the agreement. Yvonne looked after Arthur, Mary looked ter Perceval and Lynn did a superb job looking after Freddy.

T: The artists had their wives. Helen was an artist. Who was r wife?

She seemed to manage perfectly well without one.

After the lunch Mum would receive a bottle of French perfume or bunch of roses couriered as a gift from Rudy. He would know that Da would not have come to the lunch if it were not for Mum's insistence

In the next session he says to T:

Helen was equally at ease in the social gatherings of her paren social circle as she was at the art openings, the artist dinner parti I remember when we went to Sydney for the opening of an exhibitic For the first time in my life nearly all the paintings were sold. Th triumph unnerved me. If so many paintings were sold, I told myse they must be too accessible. Whatever the reason, there was som thing wrong.

The night after the opening, I had expected a quiet evening at th home of the artist friend where we were staying but it seemed that dinner party had been arranged in my honour. There was no escap I loathed these gatherings. I refused to demean myself by indulging the performance expected of an artist.

As the evening progressed, the bonhomie, the competitiveness ar the congratulations left me feeling more and more morose until th pantomime became intolerable. A woman grabbed me by the har and pulled me up from my chair announcing, 'Let's dance.'

'Let him go, Yvette,' someone said as if I was a puppet. As th guest of honour, it would have been churlish to slink off hoping n one would notice. Helen would be furious. But then, feeling more ar more ill at ease, I got up, opened the door and went outside, beyor caring if anyone noticed my departure.

I found myself walking up the hill away from the house until reached a path leading to a cliff-top. I stood there gazing down int the waves swirling below me. The pull of the waves was more tha the feeling of gravity. I glanced down every few seconds, looked awa and resumed looking at the waves. I saw myself as if outside lookir in. I was observing myself standing on the cliff-top looking dow ature was not my preferred location for a suicide. In moments of ıgst and terror which might have prompted such a deed, I made sure ere was always a painting to work on.

It seemed that I was not the only person observing. As I stood aring at the waves, I heard a man speaking to me. 'Hello there. It's all ght, it's all right.' I looked up. 'Come with me,' he said, approaching ıd taking me by the arm. Something in his demeanour put me under spell. I lost my autonomy. I did as he asked. I allowed him to take e by the arm and steer me down the hill away from the cliff-top. normally shirk at other people's touch but this time I found myself eekly surrendering.

We arrived at the front door of an unpretentious house where he ok out his keys, opened the door and directed me down the hallway ıd into the kitchen where he put the kettle on the stove.

The house felt reminiscent of the house I grew up in. The sparse diness reassured me. The light from a single globe hanging from the iling was more comforting to me than the dim light and the cultiıted bohemian disorder of the house I had fled. My host inquired if I ad children as he poured a cup of tea from a teapot dressed in a knitd tea cosy which I had not seen since childhood. A woman entered ıe room, tying the belt on her dressing gown as she sat down to join s. 'This is Marjorie,' the man told me.

Marjorie told me that they had recently become grandparents. told her about the birth of our first child and then found myself ughing at a joke I made, pleased that my host and hostess also found amusing, accepting my offer of a little gift of humour. It was not ntil after midnight when my host walked me to the place where I was aying. We shook hands. I never saw him again.

T: What drew you to this man?

He reminded me of my father. He and Marjorie were the antithsis of the artists at the dinner party. They were ordinary people ke my parents, but unlike my parents they had no expectations of me. The sound of the man's voice saying, 'It's all right, it's all rigl convinced me that at that moment it would be all right.

Neither Mother nor my father had ever come to one of my exhil tions as far as I knew. It would not matter that they didn't understan the paintings, it would have been enough that they had come.

T: You didn't want the congratulations. You wanted your paren to see the exhibition, to accept you as an artist. You put your trust i this fellow who guided you away from the cliff-top. You are puttin your trust in me. Like the man on the cliff-top, I am reassuring yo that it will be all right.

*

In the next session he says:

I trusted my instincts following the man down the cliff-top. would have served me better if I had trusted my instincts on othe occasions—like the time I was bullied into doing a portrait.

The trustees at a university wanted a double portrait of the firs chancellor and vice chancellor of the university. I said I wouldn't d it. I did not welcome the challenge of doing a double portrait, whic I had never done before. I suggested that a photograph by a profe sional photographer would be considerably cheaper but they wante a painting and apparently there was no other artist of my stature wh could do it.

One of the men was Sir Garfield Barwick, whose advice two year before to the governor-general led to the dismissal of the Whitlar Labor government. On doing my homework before the first sittin I learnt that Barwick's family was so impoverished he often walke miles to school without shoes on. He had gone to a selective-entry hig school then to university followed by a brilliant career as a barriste before becoming chief justice of the High Court. We had both com from poor families and risen to the height of our professions but, i manner I can't quite identify, Barwick let it be known that he was ɹperior to a man whose job was putting paint on canvas.

fter seeing a photo of the double portrait, I asked Mum about having ·arfield Barwick for lunch as, usually, the sitters were invited after ıe morning sitting. I wondered what a man who looked as solemn and ustere as Barwick would make of the décor of the kitchen and the ıeal Mum provided. Shopping lists, bills and gallery invitations were ropped up between the salt and pepper shakers on the kitchen table vhich would have been wiped down with a sponge. The plates were cratched floral Royal Doulton, the knives and forks well used. Mum vasn't prepared to give up her morning painting time preparing lunch ɔ she usually flung some sausages on the stove and then nipped out nd picked some lettuce and rocket from the garden to make a salad. ad provided cheese he had bought on his Monday day off.

Ie tells T:

In that awkward moment after the sitting, I invited Barwick to ınch. The offer was declined. The man who had walked several miles ɔ school, often without shoes on, had a driver waiting for him to ransport him to his next destination. It did not surprise me. Naturally, my observations of Barwick entered the portrait. On seeing the nished work Barwick reportedly said that as a work of art he didn't ave to like it. The verdict of his wife was said to be 'unprintable'. The rustees may have assumed that given my eminence as an artist and he eminence of the two men, the portrait would depict the grandiose plendour befitting a portrait of the first chancellor and vice chancellor of the university. Serves them right. I told them I didn't want to do :. I should have trusted my instincts and refused.

There's an irony to it. I had suggested a photograph instead of a ainting. A photograph of me standing with the two men sitting n front of the portrait was put into the National Portrait Gallery.

More people would see the photograph of the portrait than the ori nal in the basement of a university where it may have been demot given its reception.

T: You saw in Garfield Barwick a man who had betrayed his origi in sacking a Labor prime minister.

I know now that we cannot escape our origins. The past nev leaves us. I had thought that in not having contact with my paren I would be free of them. They wanted their sons to be successf Suddenly, at age sixty, I didn't feel the elation one might expect of successful man. Success made me feel like an impostor. I wanted hide in the studio away from the clamour demanding the next pictu When prices rose beyond what I had ever imagined, I knew there w something wrong. You'd think I would be joyously happy not havi to worry about money, but I wasn't.

T: How do you explain it?

It's an atavistic sense of guilt. It is a sin I would have to atone for. is guilt that I was so much more financially successful than my fath It was my fault for allowing it to happen.

T: You felt guilt at being more financially successful than yo father. What about your mother?

I would have thought that Mother would have enjoyed my succe as she had when I did so well at school. I remember sitting alone wh one of the children passed on the message that Mother wanted m to ring her. I had not heard from Mother for fifteen years. The une pected reference to Mother sent a nervous tremor through me. Wh could she want?

After dinner I looked up the telephone book, dialled the number ar listened apprehensively to the phone ringing. She had discovered th there was going to be a television program about me. You would thi this would be a mark of my success, a half-hour television progra about my work. She wanted to know if I was going to say somethi bad about her.

T: You wanted something more.

I should have known better. Serves me right.

the next session he says to T:

Every January Helen took the children to the beach while I stayed home painting. It's not as if I missed them, but their absence put me a limbo, waiting for their return.

One morning I had settled into painting when I remembered that I ıd left some tubes of paint inside the house. I opened the back door ıd stepped into the silence which was instantly broken by the ringing the phone. Helen always answered the phone and since she wasn't ere, it continued to ring as if daring me to pick it up. When I closed e back door to return to the studio, disconcertingly, it stopped. An ıeasiness gripped me for the rest of the day, and in the evening as valked down the path to collect the letters from the letterbox, the ought came to me, 'What if it was Mother? What if Mother was ıging, knowing Helen was away? What if she wanted to say someing to me?'

T: As long as a parent is still living, we never give up hope of reconliation. The same is true of the parent wishing to be reconciled with e child.

remember the return from the holiday at the beach. The journey ıck home brought the increasing sense of loss that the holiday was er. I remember one year coming into the kitchen and seeing Dad anding alone. There were fewer plates in the drying rack and the om seemed tidier than usual. 'Oh, so you're back,' he said, more as ı observation than a welcome home. None of us ran up to him like ıildren do in films saying, 'Daddy, we missed you.'

The holiday was not just the pleasure of the beach. It was a holiday om Dad. Mum was free of her anxiety about pleasing him, of having get back in a hurry to get his lunch. Even the sound of his voice,

'Oh, so you're back,' summoned up the apprehension that if somethi
was wrong it must be 'my' or 'our' fault.

*

He tells T:

Every year before the summer holiday I fell into a deep despor ency on the anticipation of Christmas dinner at Helen's family home will never understand why Helen insisted I come. It's not as if I was source of entertainment.

One year, three days before Christmas, I left to stay at Lindsay house. The next year I booked myself into the Southern Cross Hotel. A I entered the lobby, a sparkling Christmas tree exacerbated my mise and the sight of two young women wearing reindeer hats made m want to shake some sense into them, saying, 'There is nothing to laug about, you fatheads.'

I remember sitting in the hotel room looking at the textured wa paper, the garishly patterned bedspread, the ghastly print hanging c the wall. I imagined the room erupting in laughter, mocking me f having chosen to come here. I opened the fridge to get some ice f the whiskey I had bought but the miniature bottles of spirits shook m sense of reality as if I had fallen down the rabbit hole. I might hav escaped Helen and the prospect of Christmas dinner at her paren house but I was now held prisoner, although I could not say who was who had imprisoned me or what crime I had committed.

The next day I returned home and accompanied Helen and th children to Christmas dinner.

T: You have told me it is abject for a parent to ask a child for mone You have told me of your atavistic guilt for earning significantly mo than your father. Could it be that the request to attend Helen's paren Christmas dinner reminded you of your absence from your own pa ents on this family occasion?

I remember the Christmas day when I received the gift of the erman howitzer I had avidly looked at in the toy shop. Mother had)served how much I wanted it and bought it for me, even though it as more than she could afford.

T: You knew that your mother loved you.

I remember her disappointment when I could not take up the :holarship because she could not afford the uniform. I felt that I had iled her.

*

the next session, he says to T:

I could predict that every year I would be subjected to Helen's isistence on the Christmas dinner, but I could not have predicted er announcement that she intended teaching art classes at the CAE the evening one or two nights a week. When I asked her what she anted to do that for, she said it was to pay for the children's high :hool uniforms which were beyond her skills on the sewing machine. said that it was demeaning to teach at a place like the CAE. It was just ousewives who wanted to get out of the house, and besides, we didn't eed the money.

I assumed that would be the end of it but a few days later she asked e to sign a form confirming her credentials as an artist given my ithority as an art master at Melbourne Grammar. Naturally I refused. minute later I heard her speaking on the telephone and then I heard ie back door open and close as she left the house, presumably to get a gnature from whoever it was on the phone.

As I walked down the hallway, the sight of the scholarship painting ook me back to that moment when the winner was announced. I knew ien what I must do. I grabbed the painting at the two sides and raised up to detach the wires from the picture hooks. There was no time to appreciate the little comedy of the hooks spontaneously dancin to the floor. I took a box of matches from the stove, picked up *Th Herald* and with one hand holding the painting and the other holdin the matches and the newspaper, I pushed open the back door with m foot and steered the painting towards the backyard incinerator. Afte tossing in a few pages of the newspaper, I threw in a match. I the ripped the canvas from the frame, snapped the frame into pieces wit my foot, crumpled up the canvas, held it over the fire in an uncerem nious farewell, then allowed it to fall into the burning incinerator. watched as the flames licked their way over the formative work of m career, dissolving into ashes.

I went inside, poured myself a drink and sat in front of the tel vision before going to bed early to avoid Helen's triumphant retur with the recently acquired signature.

The next morning, the blank wall announced the deed committed i the backyard incinerator. When Helen asked me what had happene to the scholarship painting, I told her that I had burnt it, that it was m painting, I could do what I liked with it.

The painting was never referred to again until years later whe Sasha Grishin asked to see it for a book he was writing on my work. told him that I had burnt it as an inferior student work. Helen did nc contradict me.

T: You told me that you considered burning the painting in you fury at not getting the scholarship. Helen had vehemently proteste Could it be that the actual burning of the painting was vengeanc against Helen for taking a teaching job for a few nights a week?

It was my own fault. If I had not burnt the painting it would hav been hung in my retrospective exhibition. It would have proved to b a formative work which should have won the Travelling Scholarship

T: It would be vindication for not winning the prize you felt yo justly deserved.

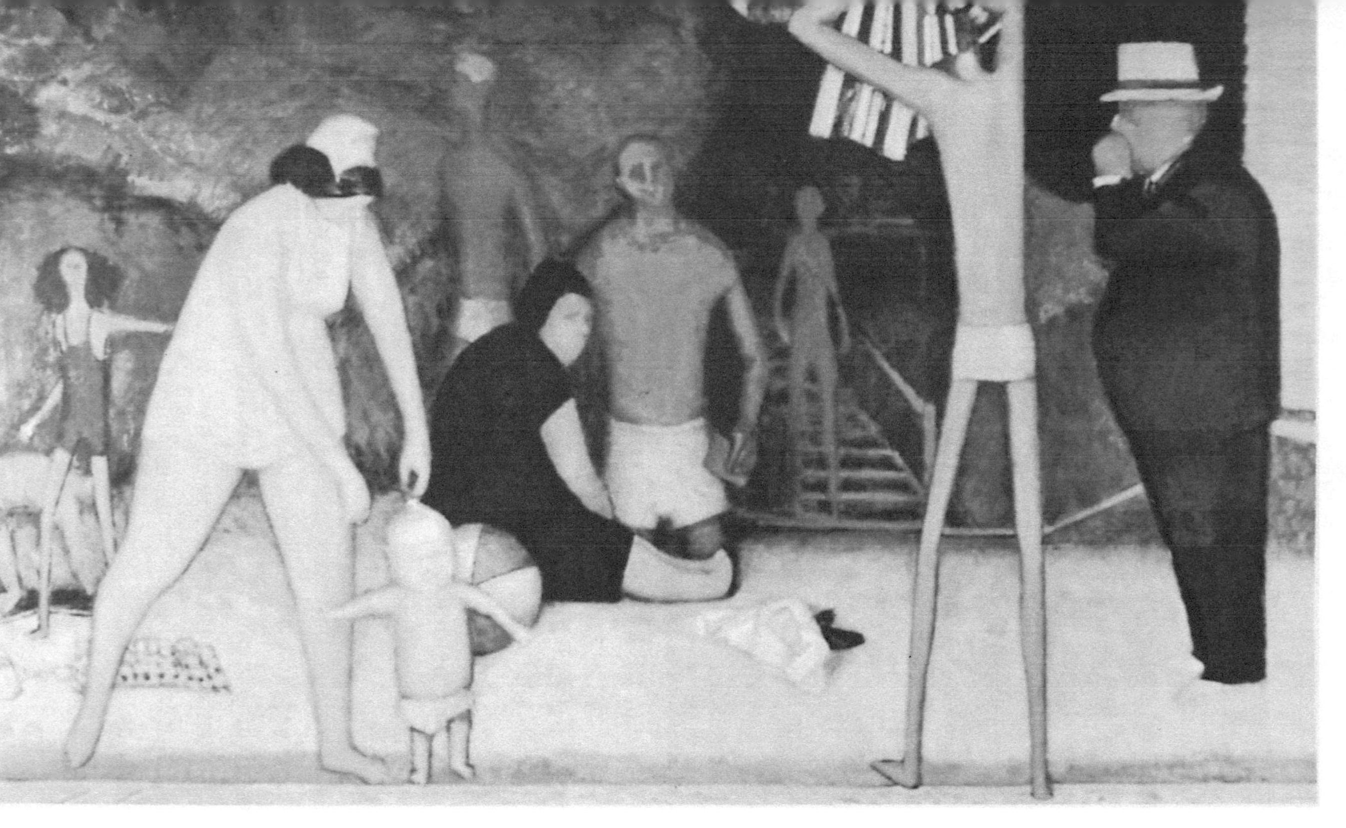

John Brack, *The Beach* 1949, oil on canvas 104.1 × 154.9 cm signature details unknown.

Mum taught evening and weekend classes at the CAE for over for years. Often at a gallery opening, a former student would approa her and tell her how much they valued her classes, how much th had learned.

He tells T:

Helen would only earn a pittance teaching at the CAE but it stru me in the middle of the night that if she could get a job, she mig leave me. Many years later when Mac took an interest in Helen's wo another fear took hold of me.

Mac and Jessie had come to lunch. After spending an hour looki at my paintings, I heard Mac ask Helen about her recent work. Ent siastically she showed Mac her paintings while I was left with t tedious task of filling in time entertaining Jessie.

That evening Helen was noticeably buoyed up by the attenti from Mac. Apparently, he had suggested putting titles on her wo 'You already have titles,' I said. He suggested longer titles that sa more about what she had told him in explaining her work.

T: What was so disconcerting about Mac's interest in Helen's wor

Mac was my friend. I had never entered Helen's painting room had never talked to her about her work. That night I lay in bed allo ing my mind to play tricks on me. What if Helen became successfu What if others took an interest in her work?

The next day at breakfast time I was jolted out of the fear th Helen's success would eclipse my own. Helen's paintings were erudi oblique, not easily accessible. She was an artist's artist. Besides, sh did not have the support of gallery directors or anybody else for th matter. As Helen handed me the plate of poached eggs, I wonder how I could have allowed myself to sink into fear.

T: You are telling me that you needed Helen to support your care but the support was not reciprocal.

ıd would probably say, 'That was her job,' but this time he doesn't.

goes on:

In the 1950s, I painted a portrait of Helen. Forty years later I inted another portrait. She was in her early sixties. 'He has painted e as quite austere, quite severe,' I heard her saying to a visitor. 'The le he has given me is, *No means no*.'

A reviewer suggested that I had painted her as 'the lighthouse in e artist's darkest moments of creative despair'.

'I mean, I ask you!' she said. 'I've never heard of anything so ridicu-ıs. A lighthouse.' She was not given to the metaphoric.

Helen was not so much a lighthouse, but a torch. Sometimes a ckering torch, sometimes a torch held with fury, sometimes an illu-inating torch. If Helen was a torch, she was also a taskmaster. Her sistence that 'no means no' sent me back into the studio when I felt e giving up.

T: What would you have done without Helen?

How would I know how to tie my shoelaces?

T: You could not have done without her.

The doctor tells me I would have drunk myself to death if Helen ıd not provided me with dinners of meat, potatoes and three vege-bles every night.

T: Are you telling me that you are grateful to Helen for keeping you ive?

Well, that was her job. I depended on her.

T: Thank you does not come naturally to you.

If 'thank you' does not come naturally to me, it came all too readily Helen. It embarrassed me when her thanks to a waiter or a nurse ere so profuse as to be condescending. Often they were spoken as e obligatory response. I remember her thank you when I gave her large bottle of expensive French perfume for her birthday. A week ter during an argument I reminded her of it.

'What rot,' she said. 'You think that's a present! It's just guilt, gu about the whiskey you buy yourself. It's the same colour. It's in a gla bottle.' She was right.

I *have* been known to say thank you. Following Helen's directiv I have made the odd phone call, written the odd thank you letter.

T: If Helen instructed you to write a thank you letter to others, sl could hardly instruct you to thank herself.

That didn't stop her seeing thanks where they were not intende In my last painting there are five figures, a larger one and four small ones. Helen sees these five figures as herself and the children. Sl sees this as my acknowledgement for all that she and the children ha done for my work. 'It was the nicest thing John ever did,' she said. Sl found what she was looking for in the painting.

T: You took Helen for granted.

I could not have painted without Helen. I could not imagine anoth woman fulfilling the role as splendidly as she did. No other perso would have had her diligence, her understanding of art, her desire f my success even more than her own.

T: What was so difficult about thanking Helen yourself?

It would have been demeaning. It would have been admitting th I could not have done it on my own.

Silence.

I did once think about it.

T: You thought about it.

We had gone shopping for a Persian rug required for painting portrait. I expected to find one at the first shop we visited but nor materialised like the one I had in mind. In my annoyance that our ta was taking far longer than I had anticipated, I found myself engulfe with frustration, irritated with Helen's driving, with the rigmarole parking the car and finding another shop.

Eventually I agreed on a rug simply for the sake of giving up c looking. When we arrived home, I remarked to Helen that it was hole day away from painting. It was a whole day away from her ainting, too, she said. It didn't matter to her one way or the other hether I found the rug I was looking for. I was the one who was look- g. I was the one who was getting increasingly disappointed. She was erely doing the driving.

On the evening walk I thought that perhaps I would say thank ou to Helen. As she said, she had given up a day of her own work help buy the rug that I needed for my work. I said to myself that hen I returned, I would say thank you. I stepped from the evening ght into the kitchen and poured myself a drink. In the familiarity of e habits of the room I could not find the words that I had rehearsed itside on the walk. Broodingly, I sat at the table waiting for my inner to be served, half-heartedly responding to Helen's attempts conversation.

T: Coming from the outside to the inside you could not find words say what you had planned.

It occurs to me now that if Helen wanted me to say thank you for hat she had done for my work, she also wanted me to say sorry for y drinking.

T: We cannot say thank you if we cannot find gratitude within us. 'e cannot say sorry if we are silenced by our shame.

Sorry, sorry, sorry.

the next session he says to T:

This pettiness about saying thank you and sorry is a way of avoid- g the more serious question.

T: What question is that?

Who am I if I am not an artist?

T: Who are you if you are not an artist?

If I am not actually painting, I am solving the problems of the ork, waiting for the solution to fall into place. I remember sitting in hrist Church, South Yarra, listening to the eulogy for Helen's mother, pondering the problem of the current painting. When the solutio occurred to me, I saw myself squeezing out of the narrow pew, runnin out of the church, getting a taxi and throwing myself into the studi I am never just posting a letter. Even when I am walking the stree of Surrey Hills, I am thinking of the problems of the work. There yo are. I have answered the question, 'Who am I when I am not an artist I am a figure in the suburban landscape.

He is a figure in my internal landscape.

One would not put one hand on Dad's arm offering sympath I never saw him put his arm around another person. A touch woul cause him to flinch. His favourite painting was Rembrandt's *Th Jewish Bride*.

He tells T:

I will always remember the first time I saw Rembrandt's paintin *The Jewish Bride*. I was looking at the most marvellous painting I ha ever seen. It's the relationship between the man and the woman. Th man inclines his head towards the woman. One of his hands prote tively touches her heart. The fingers of her hand gently touch his han in what seems like affirmation. The man and woman are not looking a each other but we are witnessing this private moment between ther It is a superb arrangement of hands. It's the touch of the man's han on the woman's heart, the touch of her hand on his hand. The woma offers no resistance to the touch. I remember the first time I saw th painting, gazing at the image, held in the aura of it.

T: In looking at the painting perhaps you were incorporating th tenderness into yourself.

Silence.

I don't know, but it did have a profound effect on me. In the mi 1950s I started on my own version of the bride and groom. I wante to show how the wedding day is the only time two people are unite s one. The next day they confront the practical decision of how to ve together.

After numerous attempts I abandoned the painting. It was all wrong. ears later, when I was picking up the children's toys, I found a little aflet from a cake-decorating set. I knew then what was needed in the ainting. It needed the wedding cake.

I had attempted the painting in dark red, burnt orange and usset, the colours in *The Jewish Bride*, but now I realised that the wentieth-century wedding demanded pale pinks, blues and yellows s shown in the little leaflet of the cake-decorating set.

As one problem was solved another had arisen. The painting eeded something else. The solution came as I glanced at the photos of ne bride and groom in the social pages of the newspaper. Little flecks f white randomly dotted the black-and-white photos as if rain had potted the photograph. I realised then that what the painting needed as confetti.

Painting is touch. The paintbrush touching the paint, the paint ouching the canvas under the masterful eye of the artist. I am a naster of touch. Never let it be said that I am a man fearful of touch. ook at the paintings.

Silence.

T: Silence is touch.

n the next session he tells T:

It seems to me that when most people look at a painting or a shop rindow, they see the object behind the glass. But when I look at something behind glass, the first thing I see is a reflection of myself.

I remember looking into a shop that sold chairs for invalids and ther sorts of props for people with disabilities. My reflection on the lass superimposed itself over the proprietor and the lady assistant who seemed to be swimming in the middle of the shop. I was struck by the peculiarity of the relationship between the people inside and r outside looking in.

T: What was peculiar about the relationship?

It seemed to me that the proprietor and his assistant were almc disembodied in the way that I felt disembodied.

T: You felt cut off from yourself.

I painted another picture of a shop window where you see a ma ikin figure of a boy standing on an oversized wheelchair. One of h legs is an artificial leg. He is smiling because he is happy to have fou the props that enable him to stand and to walk. The section of t painting where he stands is bathed in dramatic red.

T: If painting is touch, I wonder if touching the paint on canvas a prop like the artificial leg for the boy. It's a prop connecting you yourself. You become embodied when you are painting.

When I am painting, I become a happy boy.

The Happy Boy was painted mid-career. *Little Boy Lost* was paint early career.

*

Dad was on the lookout for what would solve the problem of t wedding pictures. I am on the lookout for what will explain how h conversations with T seem real. In the introduction to a collectic of Italian folktales, Italo Calvino tells us: 'Now my journey throu folklore is over...I know that this was not a hallucination, a sort professional malady, but the confirmation of something I alrea suspected—folktales are real.'

In his journey through teaching the great Russian short stori George Saunders tells us he discovered a sort of knowledge that is re but cannot be put into words. We can 'know' something but we cann ticulate what we know. The 'knowing' at such moments is real, even ough it cannot be articulated.

What I do know is that my father's conversations with T are trans- rmative. I cannot explain it. They are transformative for him and r me. They take the form of what we say when we say, 'I promise'. mething real happens in the exchanges between them.

*

continues:

I once did a series of paintings of a wooden hand that artists use a model for painting hands. I cannot recall how I got the idea to int the articulated wooden hand except that I had seen one in an art pplies shop forty years before. In order to paint the hand, I needed a odel. I went into the art material shop and was just about to ask the sistant if they had an articulated wooden hand, when I noticed that had no right hand.

I then painted the hand into a shop window with postcards bal- ced on the fingers. I was drawn to painting shop windows and if not window, a frame painted around the edge of the painting. This gives e impression that we are looking at the painting, outside looking in.

T: How did you get the idea for painting the shop window?

The idea for the shop window as a painting device came to me in 1962 ıen an image from my childhood rose unbidden in the night. It was e image of a window displaying hundreds of pocketknives and cutlery d that sort of thing. They were scattered higgledy-piggledy, as if they d been tossed in at random with no aesthetic sense of arrangement.

T: The image of the shop window had stayed with you since ildhood.

It occurs to me now that the paintings of shop windows return me that moment when I first saw the shop window with the Van Gogh int that had inspired me to paint.

T: The moment of the epiphany when you felt a tingling in the spir

Albert Camus said, 'A person's life purpose is nothing more tha to rediscover, through the detours of art or love or passionate wo those one or two images in the presence of which his heart fir opened.' Although I am known as a cerebral painter, as a 'cool detache observer', it could be said that I am seeking to return to that mome when the heart first opened.

Dad remembers the shop that sold pocketknives and cutlery. I reme ber the paintings inspired by the shop he remembered from childhoc

He continues:

The Van Gogh that I had seen in the shop window was only a pri I was considered remiss for not travelling overseas to see the paintin in the original but our own gallery, the National Gallery of Victor had a modest collection of Picassos, Rembrandts, Seurats and Modig anis. It was not until my early fifties that Helen and I planned our fir trip overseas. Right from the beginning, Helen and I disagreed on th itinerary. At one point Helen said she would stay at home, and I wou have to go alone. I said that if she didn't come, she would be deprivir me of the paintings I had wanted to see all my life.

And then what should happen when we set off? Once in the aer plane, Helen delighted in the little packaged meals delivered to her a I sunk into dejection at the sheer ordeal of the prospect of what wa to follow.

T: So what was to follow?

On the first day as we waited outside the Louvre, I wondered if th whole thing was a mistake. At the designated time, the doors opene and the crowd surged forward as if their lives would be transformed b seeing great art. Unsettled by the unexpected crowds, I found myse yearning for my natural habitat, the studio. I remember looking at th Velasquez, thinking, 'Is it worth all the effort to get here?'

T: You had not anticipated the number of tourists.

I had expected the aura of the painting in the flesh, not the crowds ' other tourists flocking to the gallery at the same time as we were. was naïve of me to imagine that I would be looking at the paintings one just because art was my profession. A 'great' gallery gives the aintings within it the mystique of Great Art. These tourists would not ok twice if they saw the same paintings in a little gallery up a dead-nd laneway. It was not just the bobbing of other people's heads in ont of the painting, neither was it the subdued chatter...these large ssemblies of *grand peintures* were hung as if they were proclaiming, ook at me. Look at me. I am a genius. I am a hero.' It is not the fault of e artist. It is the curators, the gallery directors and the critics who t the finished work out of the mundane ordinariness of the artist's udio into the glitter of the Kingdom of Art.

Overwhelmed by the clamour of 'look at me', 'the artist as hero', I ed downstairs where I found the work of the Egyptians, Sumerians nd Assyrians. There I had the opportunity to look at them intently ithout the encumbrance of other bodies and without the proclama-ons of the greatness of the work.

One would think that I would have learnt my lesson after the ouvre but the same thing happened when visiting the Rijksmuseum Amsterdam. We had gone there to see *The Jewish Bride* but the normity of the crowds sent me retreating downstairs to the basement. ne silent dignity of the Buddhist statue *Guanyin Avolokiteshva* made *he Jewish Bride* look vulgar.

I had set out on the journey to look at the paintings only to discover e obstruction and the fascination with other people not looking at e paintings. Tourists flocked to the gift shops buying postcards of hat they had not really seen. It's the existential dread. The need have something in one's hand, a souvenir, something to show for it. bought some of the postcards myself knowing I would do something ith them, but not knowing what.

T: So the whole expedition did not fulfil what you had imagined would.

To make things worse, right from the beginning it seemed that was prepared to take a more leisurely approach than Helen. As sh revelled in the galleries I was wishing to return to the familiarity the studio. Exhausted by the crowds in front of the paintings, I su gested wandering the city as flâneurs. At first she objected but then a she came to marvel at the shops, the parks, the people, I just wanted t get back to the hotel.

T: Let me get this right. Helen didn't want to go on the oversea expedition but you said you wouldn't go without her. When sh agreed to come, she enjoyed it and you sulked at the ordeal. Instea of being gratified that Helen had found enjoyment in the trip you ha manipulated her into taking, you punished her for her enjoyment as disgruntled, surly travelling companion.

He says nothing.

Instead of succumbing to disappointment at his trip overseas, Dad di something imaginatively with the postcards he had bought. He copie them into his paintings, balancing them on knives and forks. He aske the three grandchildren to paint a picture of a king or queen on a blan postcard he had given them. He then painted their postcards in th same composition as the postcards of kings and queens painted b the great masters.

On returning from their trip overseas, Mum told me that when the were in Paris Uncle Lindsay had rung to tell Dad that their mothe had died.

'How did Daddy respond to hearing of his mother's death?' I aske

'Well, it was nothing really.'

'He must have felt sad or sorry or something.'

'No, he didn't. John wasn't like that.'

'He wasn't like what?'

'He wasn't sentimental.'

In my last year at school, we read *The Outsider* by Albert Camus 'anslated from the French. It starts with, 'Mother died today. Or ıaybe it was yesterday, I don't know.'

ı the next session he says to T:

I didn't tell you what else happened on that trip overseas. On the ıte afternoon of our third day in Paris, I returned to the hotel room 'hile Helen did some shopping. I was glad to have the time alone but ıis meant that when the telephone rang it was incumbent on me ɔ pick it up. I allowed it to ring, thinking it would stop, but when it ontinued, I answered, expecting the hotel receptionist. It was Lindsay peaking from the other side of the world. My ears must have been eceiving me, I thought, or someone was playing a trick on me or must have been dreaming.

'Mother died today,' he said.

A guttural cry escaped me.

'I thought you should know,' Lindsay said, as if apologising for ıterrupting what he would have considered a holiday.

I offered to return for the funeral, knowing he would not expect me ɔ return. After putting down the phone I stumbled to the armchair nd sat down staring at the rosy patterned wallpaper, amused by the ttle comedy of hearing of Mother's death from inside a forest of tiny ɔsebuds. Shortly after, Helen returned.

'I just met this marvellous man and I bought this divine cheese nd...'

'Mother died today,' I said. 'I don't remember whether Lindsay said ɔday" or "yesterday"; besides, the time difference would mean that if was today here, it would be yesterday there or vice versa.'

In niggling over the day of Mother's death, I was avoiding what I idn't want to face: the fact of Mother's death. I wanted to be alone.

I told Helen I wanted to go out for a walk to the little park seve blocks along the street. I stepped from the hotel and walked along t street comforted that I would not run into anyone I knew. I reach the park and sat down on one of the impractical little decorative chai where I replayed Lindsay's words, 'Mother died today.' Time took a new dimension. The sky turned a darker shade of blue, people we returning from work or going out for the evening. Every one of the human beings has a mother, I thought. Every one of these hum beings loves and hates his mother.

As I sat there in the evening light, I found myself rummagi through memories of Mother. I remembered the toy gun from Fath Christmas, knowing that Mother had found the money for it ev though she could not afford it. I remembered sitting at the kitch table doing my homework while Mother did the ironing. I remember flinging words in her direction, 'vicarious', 'desultory', 'decrepitu 'elucidate', knowing she would not know the meaning.

I remembered Mother's pride when I won the scholarship Ivanhoe Grammar and her subsequent disappointment that she cou not afford the uniform for me to go there. I remembered feeling p tective of Mother at the excruciating engagement party where Heler mother talked about the difficulty of getting good 'help'. I remember Mother's delight when her first grandchild was born, a girl she h always wanted. I remembered the last time I spoke to Mother. It w on the phone. Neither of us said goodbye.

As I retraced my steps along the boulevard, I determined not to lured into talking about Mother, knowing Helen's justifiable hostili to her. She was my mother.

I returned to the hotel room where Helen had arranged the divi cheese on a sheet of butcher's paper and had somehow procured knife. Earlier that day we had looked at Manet's *Lunch on the Gra* Now we were actually having dinner in a forest of rosebuds, inward absorbed in vastly different worlds, unknown to the other.

The next day as we entered the Galerie Orsay, I realised that outardly everything looked the same—the queues outside the gallery, e cars driving around Paris. Yet something had irrevocably changed side me.

T: Talking about your mother's death has revived your love and te for your mother.

*

ıd was inventively confident in his paintings but he was not so conlent in the practical tasks of dealing with his children. One Saturday orning when Mum was out shopping, I tumbled and fell from my ke. Blood trickled from a cut on my leg but I managed to get back my bike and ride home. I intended to clean the wound myself, but ıd happened to be leaving the bathroom as I went in. 'I fell off my ke,' I said, explaining why I was entering the bathroom as he was aving. I sat on the edge of the bath while Dad frantically searched the medicine cupboard for a bandage. I probably said sorry for the ouble I was causing, taking him away from painting.

There is no reason for him to remember the experience, but if he oes, this is how he reports it to T:

ıe morning when Helen was out shopping, one of the children rushed to the bathroom, blood dripping from her leg. She had fallen from r bike, she said. The sight of blood trickling from her leg threw me to a panic. Helplessly, I opened the medicine cupboard, only to be nfronted by a jumbled forest of medicine bottles, pills and cottonool. Having found the bandage, I discovered it was in one long piece quiring a pair of scissors to cut it shorter. Helen had done nothing sensible as to have the scissors nearby, so I scurried into our bedom to her sewing machine and hunted around the mess of fabrics ıd pins to locate her dressmaking scissors. Eventually I managed to cut a bandage and then, having fumblingly dabbed the wound wi mercurochrome, I placed the bandage over the open wound and the relocated everything into the cabinet as best I could. With the reli of one who no longer has to sing a song he doesn't know the words I escaped into the studio.

T: You escaped into the studio.

I was escaping from having to do something I was not practised doing.

T: You were escaping from the ordeal of finding a bandage ar putting it on a child's wound.

I was escaping the flesh and blood. Painting is my flesh and blooc

Long silence.

There was one other time when I felt compelled to escape into tl studio.

T: What were you seeking to escape?

The grief over Freddy's death. I have often replayed the mome I heard that Freddy had cancer and not long to live. He was on fifty-four. His wife Lynn and three teenage daughters were losing husband and father, but I was losing my closest friend.

Immediately after Freddy's death I wrote the eulogy for his funer I remember saying, 'The death of the artist is different from the deat of others. While he lives the artist is his work, and when he dies, l stays behind. This is the great consolation both to the artist and those who are left. The artist is his work.'

For me, the work was not sufficient consolation. Helen and tl children wisely knew not to refer to Freddy's death. Nothing wa spoken in the family until six months later on Christmas day. Aft dinner the children chatted innocuously as I sat there glumly un called upon to speak. Then, out of this cacophony, I heard Freddy name. The children were speaking their reminiscences. They recalle how he gave them chocolate Freddo frogs when he was babysittir how Freddy and I once played shuttlecock in the back garden muc their amusement. Then, after a lull in the reminiscences, a peculiar ound emerged from the footstool where the first daughter was sitting the end of my chair. I assumed it was laughter about something she membered of Freddy but then I realised it was the sound of weeping. grown-up daughter sobbing, right there on the little footstool near y feet.

Instinctively I rose from my chair and left the room but after tching more ice for the whiskey there was nowhere to sit. I could ot return to my chair so near to this weeping, so I had no alternative ut to roam the hallway restlessly, putting my head in the doorway peating to no one in particular, 'Why is Clara crying? Freddy was y friend.'

By the time they were leaving she had recovered from her weeping. sually, I hover in the background hoping to avoid the perfunctory ss but this time I found myself lurching towards the weeping daugh- r, throwing my arms around her, grasping her to me as tightly as all y strength permitted. After letting go, she stared at me speechless, asping for breath. I do not know what overcame me.

T: You could not weep at the death of your dearest friend so your aughter took it on herself to do the weeping for you. The attempt at nbrace was your attempt at acknowledgement.

do not know if that is the explanation. Nothing was ever spoken of it. remember thinking for half a second that Dad was coming to give me hug, but the hug turned out to be an almost suffocation.

Another memory of tears returns to me. This time I was trying to onceal the tears. I was six or seven years old. Dad was drawing my ortrait. I was trying with all my effort to sit perfectly still, thinking hat if I moved, he would make a mistake. He must have noticed my ears for I remember him saying, 'You can move, you know.'

Nearly thirty years later, he did portraits of the four of us daugh- ers. Mum had gone overseas. He refused to go with her. I remember preparing for the sitting thinking, 'I will not see him as the omnipoter father. I will not see him as the observer like the man on the beach i the scholarship painting.' I remember composing myself respectfull sitting on the chair looking at him a few feet away, his pencil sketchin lines on his drawing pad. As I watched him look at me, put the penc on the paper, drawing a line, it occurred to me that's all a portrait i one pencil line after another.

After the sitting I helped him put together the lunch. Mum alway managed the conversation so now that she wasn't here it was up t me to ask Dad questions about art. It never occurred to me to tell hi what was going on in my life. I do remember him taking a Nabok novel from his bookshelf, 'You might like this,' he said. I took this as a offer to connect.

A professional photographer took several photographs of Da sitting in the studio with the portraits behind him. We were show the set of photographs and asked to select one. Later I regretted nc picking a photograph that was more characteristic of him. I ha chosen one of him smiling as I had imagined the photographe had instructed.

He says to T:

I had drawn pictures of the children when they were very young. named the pictures *First Daughter, Second Daughter, Third Daughte* and *Fourth Daughter*. When Helen went overseas one summer holida I drew portraits of them again, now they were in their thirties. Thi time I gave them their names, *Portrait of Clara/Vicky/Freda* an *Charlotte*.

T: You chose the time to do the portraits when Helen was oversea

It would give me some connection with them without Helen' interference.

I remember drawing each daughter's head, doing the chit-cha required for anyone sitting for their portrait. I remember sketching i ne daughter's eyes realising that I knew very little about her. I knew ıore about my students at the art school. The relief when she left was ke when any sitter left. Now I could get on with my real work back ı the studio. This time the relief was accompanied by the sense of aving missed something.

T: What had you missed?

That moment of drawing their portraits would never be repeated. hat is the closest I will ever get to my children. I knew nothing about irls. I had one brother. It's not just that they were girls. How could I et to know them? I was busy in the studio. Never did we do anything ɔ much as toss a ball between us. Our paths crossed as we went in r out of a room. When they were little, they were more like encumrances. Their toys were strewn around the floor and when they were lder there was the petty bickering, and then their miseries that didn't oncern me. How could I have a conversation with any one of them iven their ignorance about the world?

Then there were the tantrums and Helen's petty worries about ıem, worries that she attempted to inflict onto me and which I satisıctorily avoided. Maybe none of us know our children. Did Tolstoy now his children? How could he get to know his children if he was ʋriting *War and Peace*?

Long silence.

My children have grown up with my paintings on the walls. They now me from the paintings. I may not know very much about them, ut they know me in a way that I do not know myself.

had always understood that we didn't see much of Dad because he ʋas so busy painting, but it wasn't until Mum's response to our time ʋith him in hospital that I wondered if there was another reason for ur distance from our father.

He was in hospital recovering from a prostate operation. The urses could not be expected to sit with a patient with dementia so

Mum drew up a roster for the four of us to take turns sitting with h
when she could not be there herself. It required holding him back fro
pulling at the catheter, stopping him from wrestling his way out
the hospital gown, explaining that he was in hospital, not in a ho
preparing to give a speech. It required thinking up a topic that mig
inspire conversation.

When Mum arrived at 10.30 pm ready to take over for the night
was eager to get home but she demanded that I stay. She wanted
demonstrate her caring technique, proving its superiority to mi
Stroking Dad's face she repeated, 'It's all right lambie pie, I am he
There, there lambie pie.' The bleak desperation of the repeated 'lamb
pie' was unbearable.

Another time I had only just arrived when she told me that r
face was lopsided, one side looking swollen. She wondered wheth
I had cancer. I understood the stress of looking after Dad, the ang
at seeing him with dementia, the responsibility of caring for him wi
barely a moment to herself—but why would she create anxiety in n
suggesting I had cancer when I was only trying to help?

Mum had no choice but to roster us to look after Dad. Her reactio
wasn't sympathetically, 'I know how hard it is. It must be confronti
seeing your father in this state.' It was, 'There you all are, swanning
to see your father.' As she saw it, we were not rushing to the hospit
from the other side of town after work in peak-hour traffic havi
grabbed something for dinner. We were 'swanning in'.

Over the years I had gleaned that Mum longed to have some mea
ingful connection with *her* father but now I wondered whether s
may have felt threatened if we had some connection with our own.

After Dad's death, I offered my condolences, sympathising wi
Mum's loss, knowing her struggle looking after him. I acknowledg
her grief. She conveyed no sense that I had 'lost' a father, not that
was a wonderful father, but he *was* my father. The mourning was
hers. He belonged to her.

When Mum suggested that we were swanning in to see our father, e phrase 'swanning in' suggested that perhaps there was another ɔry about Dad's distance from us children. Perhaps it was not Dad ıo wanted to be kept away from his children; perhaps it was Mum ıo would rather we not have a relationship with our father. 'Swanng in' suggested an Oedipal attachment, 'courting' our father. I did a ıick sort through my memories of our experience with Dad to see if ould identify any other clues as confirmation.

Dad chose to do our portraits when Mum was overseas. When I erheard him saying to Mum, 'Of course I am only doing the chilen's portraits as practice for Ursula,' I was hurt. Weren't we worthy having our portraits drawn, just in being his daughters? Perhaps he ıs reassuring Mum that he didn't really want to spend time with us, was all just practice for a more important person.

I recall the Christmas dinner when Mum went overseas. We usually ıve the dinner in the dining room. This time Dad set up a long trestle ble in his studio. He had cooked the meal himself with some considable assistance. He was actually smiling and seemed pleased with mself for making us this offer. We were in his territory, the studio. emember the Christmas decorations around the room.

'There you are, swanning in to see your father.' I wondered if Mum ared we had the same attachment to Dad that she had. She is the ife. We are the children. Art was their joint work together.

I can hear Mum saying, 'No, that's just rubbish.'

ıe next session he says to T:

After more than a decade teaching at Melbourne Grammar, I was ked to be head of the National Gallery art school, the school where I ıd studied. I said that I would only do it if I had a studio and only for few years until they could find a more permanent replacement.

In the first week after starting work I walked through the city, ancing in the shop windows reorienting myself, when I found myself staring at a display of pens. I decided to buy an expensive founta pen which I could now afford with the full-time salary I was earning

I selected a wine-red pen with gold trimming. The shop assista demonstrated how to fill it and then handed me a writing pad on whic were scrawled the cursive scripts of others before me, *Carpe die The rain in Spain stays mainly on the plain, Happy birthday*. I mac my contribution *Garlic and sapphires in the mud*. The shop assista then produced a box with gold trimming lined with royal-blue velv He placed the pen into the groove, shutting the box with a silent thu He then asked if it was a gift and when I said no, he put it into a brow paper bag.

A year later the question, 'Is it a gift?' returned when my fir daughter left school and was about to go to university. I had bee thinking of buying her a gift as a rite of passage. Helen organised th presents for birthdays and Christmas, so this was my opportunity assert myself as a father.

I went into the shop and selected the same pen as the one I ha bought myself. The shop assistant put it into its blue velvet crib ar when he asked if it was a gift, I assured him that indeed it was. I no had the opportunity to observe him meticulously wrapping the bc in gold-and-red-striped wrapping paper, completing the performanc with the flourish of a red bow.

When I got home, I put the parcel on the coffee table. There wa something not quite right about the wrapping paper. The exquisi careful wrapping looked uncharacteristic of something I would giv I undid the bow and then proceeded to rip off the wrapping pape knowing that in two seconds I had wrecked what the fellow in th shop had taken five minutes to perfect.

I then opened the box and gazed at the fountain pen. The royal-blu velvet box gave it a regal pretension, more like a gift Helen's fami would give. I lifted out the pen and held it in my hand. It was glear ingly new, not marked with little scratches like my own.

A few hours later, my daughter came into the room where I was sit-ng alone. I put down the book I was reading, swivelled around to the ɔokshelf behind me, grabbed the pen and thrust it in her direction, ɜaring myself say, 'Take this. I bought it for myself. I don't use it any-.ore. You might as well have it. And take this ink,' I added, handing ver the unopened bottle.

The effusiveness of her thanks was noticeably greater than was arranted for something I had bought for myself and didn't use ıymore.

T: After your good intentions you thrust the pen at your daughter s if it was any old thing you no longer needed, a cast-off.

I knew then why I wanted to give this gift. I had not received a gift ke this from my father. Leaving school at fifteen and a half was not a ıuse for celebration; it was a rebuke to my father for not being able to ford to keep me at school, especially since my teachers had urged me stay for my academic potential. Keeping my children at school was sign of my success as a father.

T: You wanted to give your daughter what your father did not give you, but because he had not given it to you, your resentment stopped ɔu from giving it with the generosity with which it was intended.

For the very reason that my father did not give me a gift on leaving chool, I wanted to give one to my daughter. But because he had not .ven me this gift, I did not know how to give it.

Fifteen years after handing over the pen, I received a letter from ıy daughter, scolding me for what she saw as my negligence as a ıther. She drew attention to the fact that the letter was written with ıe fountain pen I had claimed that I no longer needed. I replied to her tter with the pen that I had bought for myself.

wo days after posting the letter, I noticed an envelope addressed to ıy husband in my father's handwriting. 'Why is he writing to Ross?' wondered. I looked again. It was addressed to 'Mrs Ross Williams'.

My father had addressed the envelope to me in my husband's name. had also written a letter to my mother and a joint letter to both of ther

Dad wrote back suggesting that I was 'troubled' and if there wa anything to do to help, he would. Many years later, when he was i hospital with dementia, he told me that the doctor had written a lette to Mum. 'Oh,' I said, 'what did it say?'

He glared at me. 'It was like that letter you wrote to me, so *scoldin*

In the many hours of crafting the letter, I thought I had conceale my anger at him. I reread my copy of it. He was right. It was scolding

He tells T about my letter:

One day, unexpectedly, I received a letter from my first daughter. read the letter once, just enough to get the gist of it. When I realise she was roughly the same age as I was when I painted *The Return* *the Prodigal Son*, I knew then that the letter was not for me, it was fo her. It was for her to express her anger at me for my failings as a fathe

Helen had also received a letter. I had no inclination to tell her wha was in mine and presumed that her letter expressed the same incrim nating disappointment.

After some fussing about, wanting to tell me and avoiding what sh wanted to tell me, Helen told me what she didn't want to tell me. stranger had taken our daughter to the creek bed at the bottom of th hill where we lived. He had raped her.

I could not bear to think about it. The brutality of men in the arm upset me. As a boy I could not tolerate fights in the school yard. wanted to banish the thought from my mind. A rape was too awfu to contemplate. I did the sums. I told Helen that by my calculation, happened almost twenty-five years ago, plenty of time to get over it.

I returned to the studio somewhat rattled. After three attempts a painting, I put down the paintbrush, washed the brushes and walke up the street intending to buy another bottle of whiskey in case I ra out. I needed to find a way of dealing with Helen's response. She woul lame herself, 'I tried so hard to do the right thing.' She would blame ur daughter, 'Why didn't she tell us before?' She would berate herself, told the children over and over never to speak to strange men.'

On the way home from the bottle shop, I considered how to deal ith Helen's response. I knew she would not let it go. On arriving ack home, I scurried over to the shadows under the tree near the back nce, wondering how to tell Helen that I didn't want to know what appened any more than she did. I dug up the leaves with my bare ands, making a shallow grave for the whiskey bottle and as I rumpled ie leaves, concealing the bottle, the thought came to me, 'It didn't appen.' The problem of Helen's distress had been solved.

I returned to the studio repeating to myself, 'It didn't happen, it idn't happen.'

With renewed energy, I focused on painting for the remainder of ie afternoon. At 5 pm I paused at the flywire door, rehearsing my eclaration. When I stepped inside the kitchen, I was surprised to see lelen holding a glass vase, swivelling a tea towel into the centre of it ı a way I had never seen before. 'It didn't happen,' I said. After a few ack-and-forth remarks about whether it did or did not happen, we et the matter rest. The next morning, Helen had come to her senses. : was never mentioned again.

T: Do you believe that your daughter was raped?

She could not have made it up. She wasn't prone to telling lies. could not bear to think about it.

T: In telling Helen that it hadn't happened you were telling her that ou were not willing to listen to her concerns about it.

My exhibition was in two months.

ı the year of the rape, Dad painted *The Chase*, a painting of three of s children running. I remember the dresses. Granny, Mum's mother, ought them from Georges. Mum didn't like the Peter Pan collars so close to the neck, so she cut them off with the scissors, scooping c the necks.

In the next session he says to T:

I do not know why my daughter felt she had to tell Helen what h pened at the creek bed. When we wrote letters home from the arr we protected our parents from what distressed us. We put it all behi us. No soldier would consider telling his parents what happened wh he returned home.

T: So what did happen in the army?

The humiliation of the first night in the army jolted me into seei how ill-prepared I was for the company of men. My literacy a aptitude for maths meant that I was rapidly promoted. It was my j to hand out the letters from home. One day in the silence after distr uting the letters, I happened to look up from reading my own lett when I noticed a fellow glancing towards me, one of the fellows w had mocked me for my poetry books, threatening to tear it to pieces knew then what he wanted. I motioned him to follow me outside, a it was there behind the mess hall that I read aloud the letter from h girlfriend, and it was there the next day that he dictated his letter response.

Not all letters from wives and girlfriends expressed the san devotion. One day the quiet reading was shattered by the sound of gunshot. A soldier had shot himself in the head. Only moments befo I had handed him his letter. Instinctively, I found myself reading t open pages he had left. His fiancé had written to tell him she was ve sorry, but she was marrying another man.

T: It was not your fault. There was nothing you could have done prevent it.

It's the futility of his death. He was only twenty-one, a boy. It w the futility of war. It was the wastefulness of life, not just his life b those whose lives were lost by the killing in war. We weren't even hting in battle. We were soldiers in training. I couldn't bear it.

T: Who knows what else was going on in the life of that young an? Who knows what other troubles he carried from his childhood? was not your fault.

ho knows what other troubles my father carried from his childhood? told me about the shooting in the army but there must be other iumas he did not tell. I invent a single event that represents all that kept hidden.

says to T:

One morning when I was still a schoolboy, I noticed a brown paper g concealed in the privet hedge near the front fence. It appeared to ive been shoved into the hedge by someone passing in the street as if sted anonymously into the hedge instead of the letterbox. Curious know what was in it, I pulled it out and opened it up but then closed I looked again. I didn't want to know. I put it back where I found it. I ntinued walking to school, wondering if I had really seen what I had en. I thought I had done something wrong, but I didn't know what was.

All day the image reappeared before me. A newborn or not-t-born baby, dead. I could not understand how it had got there. I membered overhearing Mother saying something about Mrs Jelbart er the road having had a 'backyard abortion'. I understood it was rong. I wondered if the baby was something to do with an 'abortion'.

I was frightened. I thought I should tell someone, but there was no ie I could tell. When I got back home, the paper bag had gone. I could etend to myself that I had never seen it but I knew that I had.

T: You saw something you didn't understand. You kept that iowledge to yourself. You connected to the fear that you had done mething wrong but didn't know what it was.

I did not understand what made me conjure up this image to represe what I did not know about Dad's childhood. It did not seem like son thing that would happen.

Another memory came back to me. Mum told us that she had give birth to twins very prematurely. All I knew was that they died.

He tells T:

Nine months after Freda was born, Helen became pregnant wi twins, a girl and a boy. They both died, born prematurely.

T: That must have been very distressing, especially for Helen.

She didn't talk about it.

T: As you had not talked about that glimpse of the baby in th paper bag, Helen had not talked about the death of the twins. As yc had no experience of being listened to, you had no capacity to liste to Helen.

You are listening to me. I am listening to myself. Hand on my hea

*

I am wondering where to go from here. I started with the intentic of finding compassion for my father. I had hoped it was compassic for him that stopped me from taking the photograph of him on o Sunday walk. I remembered a story told by the writer James Ellrc The detectives had botched the investigation into the murder of h mother, so he decided to take a break from writing to do his own inve tigation. Some time into his investigation, he realised that it wasn't h mother's murderer he needed to find. He needed to find out abo his mother's life before she was so brutally taken from him.

My intention was to find compassion for my father. Perhaps n real need is for *him* to find compassion for his mother.

As far as I know, Dad made no attempt to contact his mother ar she made no attempt to contact him. Surely a mother would long

·e her child before she died. I remembered Maria who was in the ›spital bed next to mine.

I give my experience of Maria to my father.

e tells T:

Last week I was in hospital for a routine procedure. Maria was in ıe bed next to mine. 'Why she not come? Why she not come?' she ılled after pressing the button for the nurse. I assured her that the ırse would come when she was ready.

At visiting hours Maria's daughter arrived and I could hear mother ıd daughter conversing in Greek, more like bickering than a conver- ıtion. After a long, expressive monologue from Maria, followed by a ·ief reply from her daughter, the daughter emerged from behind the .ue curtain.

'She is driving me mad. I'm not coming to see her again.'

After the daughter left, I thought I should say something to Maria, for no other reason than to let her know that the monologue had ıterrupted my reading.

'So that was Toula, your daughter,' I said.

'Yes,' said Maria, and then her voice raised to a kind of bleating, ut why he not come? Why he not come?' Thinking she had got her ·onouns mixed up, I told her the nurse would come when she was ·ady. It wasn't the nurse she wanted. It was her son. 'Peter, my son. 'hy he not come?' It was pitiful, a grown woman calling for her son.

T: You saw Maria and you saw your mother longing to see you.

If that is how the mother speaks to her daughter, the son has the ›od sense not to see her.

The next day the blue curtain was pulled back to reveal Maria tting on the bed ready to go home. She was dressed in a nondescript ‹irt and a grey windcheater imprinted with a large pink heart. A man .most twice her size arrived and, without looking at her, mumbled a ·w words in Greek as he picked up her suitcase. In his floor-length billowing black dress and heavy silver cross dangling around his nec he majestically led the way with Maria behind him—a frail creatur grasping her handbag in one hand and the red carnations her daughte had given her in another.

'Goodbye Maria,' I said. 'I wish I was going home.'

T: You saw the disdain in the priest and you saw yourself. You ar seeking to find compassion for your mother. You are seeking to fin compassion for yourself.

I want to believe that he is able to hear what T is saying. But then wha does he do? He flees the scene of the revelation as if it was a crime h had committed. It is too much for him to take in.

In the next session he says to T:

I don't know why I am here. I know now that I am not mad althoug I have always feared insanity. I should be back in the studio, paintin Helen will be wondering where I am. She probably has the dinne ready for me.

T: This is your response to my suggestion that you are seeking t find compassion for your mother, compassion for yourself.

When I was at the gallery school, my secretary came in offerin her unsolicited opinion on the painting I was doing. 'I suppose you experiences in the war make you paint like that,' she said. 'I was jus as morbid before the war,' I said.

I am still morbid. I don't know the origin and even if I did, I wouldn tell you. I may be morbid, but I am not mad. What is it with all thi talking? It is pure self-indulgence. And besides, it's not as if you ar telling me truths about the world like Heidegger's theory of bein There is nothing more you can extract from me. If I was going to d a picture of this, I would call it *Nothing. Nothing to be done.* I hav finished. Is man no more than this? No, I have a better idea. I will call i *Exit*. Time for my departure. Time to end these sessions. I am leaving

T: Let us continue for another four weeks as a transition to ending ur sessions.

Four weeks will be more than sufficient.

he next session he comes in hobbling on crutches, his leg in plaster. e says to T:

As you can see, I have broken my leg. I stumbled and fell into a othole in the pavement.

T: Just as you are thinking of leaving our sessions you repeat the ct that led you here in the first place.

I used to be fascinated by a single artificial leg in a shop window I assed as a student on the way to the gallery school. As far as I could ee, there was nothing else in the shop but every time I passed the indow, I saw a man peeping out. I never failed to look in the window nd he never failed to look out.

Twenty years later when I returned to the gallery school, I tried o find the shop, but it was no longer there. It had been replaced by nother surgical supply shop nearby. I knew that I must paint the nore recent shop window, but before that I would paint the memory f the window that had left such a strong impression on me.

T: What was it about the single artificial leg that had left such a trong impression on you?

The single prosthetic leg in the shop window presented itself like n object in a museum. I was influenced by the French philosopher ndré Malraux who wrote *The Museum Without Walls*. The single rosthetic leg represented the existential terror of the individual seeking purpose in life. It amused me to imagine a man hobbling along on ne leg and passing the shop window, saying ecstatically, 'That is just hat I wanted.' Originally, I called the painting *Artificial Limb-maker's hop* but when I realised I had inadvertently solved the problem of the liché of the still life of the bowl of fruit and flowers, I renamed it *Still ife with Artificial Leg*.

See! he says, pointing to his leg. This is *Still Life with Plastered L* Or *Leg Stilled in Plaster*.

T laughs.

The leg appeared to me as a lost object, a leg looking for a co panion leg, a dancer looking for the dance. When I put the finishi touches on the anonymous man in the window looking out, I realis I was that man. The artist hides himself in the painting. He is insi the painting, looking out.

T: If the artist hides himself in the painting, where are you hidi now that you are no longer painting?

There is nowhere to hide, least of all, talking to you. The unco scious is the only other hiding place I know.

T: As I said in the first session, the artist is like a child playing game of hide and seek. It is a joy to be hidden but a disaster not to found.

Perhaps it was a bit premature to suggest leaving our sessions.

T: Let us consider your capacity to repair your relationship wi your mother and your father, to repair your relationship to yours What would it take for you to make these reparations?

*

One of Dad's paintings is on the cover of *The Vivisector*, a novel Patrick White. The publisher gave him a copy. Dad passed it onto n 'I can't read it. You might as well have it.'

I read David Marr's biography of Patrick White. I recognised n father—the talent, the dedication to the work, the desire for vin cation of early negative reviews, the gap between one's sense oneself and the exalted image others have of the writer, the arti the relationship with failure, the shame, the cruelty to the supporti partner, the reclusiveness, the self-loathing. Patrick White is quot saying, 'My flawed self has only ever felt intensely alive in the tions I create.'

says to T:

It's a wonder I have not thought of this before. What if I do a rtrait of you? It would present me with my greatest challenge, tackg the problem of a portrait of a person who is completely unknown me. Maybe the struggle of this painting will allow me to repair yself, following your instructions.

T: Where would you start, with the head or with the feet?

I would start with what I know, the Persian carpet, more specifilly the flaw in the Persian carpet. My flawed self is never more fully ive than in the paintings I create. What an opportunity. Two flawed lves sitting opposite each other.

I had painted a portrait of Tam Purves, the director of a gallery here I exhibited my work. He liked it so much he asked me to paint e of his wife, his co-director, who was very good at the business de of it. Artists feel somewhat beholden to the gallery directors who hibit their work so I agreed to do it although I was not really keen do so.

When Anne saw her finished portrait, her response was uncenred, undisguised. I believe that when she showed it to her mother, r mother burst into tears. 'You, of all people, should know that my rtraits are not pretty,' I said. 'What did you expect? The Mona Lisa?'

A few months later I heard that the painting was included in an ction catalogue under the title *Woman in a Blue Suit*. 'The painting a portrait,' I wrote back. My reputation was at stake. It was withawn from auction and I thought nothing more about it.

Some time later I learned that it had not been stored in one of the any places a painting could be stored by a couple who own an art llery. It had been burnt in a little ceremony in their 44-gallon barrel um in the backyard. They had attempted to conceal the sale at auction but they wanted me to know about the burning. They want to punish me. I could have told them the repercussions of burning painting. The burning does not get rid of the offending item. It draw attention to the motivation for the need to destroy it.

T: You remembered the burning of a portrait just as you consider painting my portrait. If you painted my portrait, are you worried th I wouldn't like it, that I would burn it, that my mother would bur into tears?

I am worried that it would reveal too much of myself reflected bac

One day as I was leaving a visit to my parents, my father sa pompously to my fourteen-year-old and twelve-year-old daughte 'Cézanne said, "I have failed to realise my sensations." Life is a seri of defeats.'

He says to T:

I am worried that I am too like my father. Working in the facto my father was a defeated man. He did not keep his defeat to himse He passed it onto me like a gambler passing on a wad of notes an envelope under the table. By the time I realised what was in th envelope it was too late to return it. The artist's work is inherently o of defeat. The artist never lives up to his ambition.

When Lindsay told me that Pater had died, I put down the pho and poured myself a drink. It was not until I heard myself telli Helen that the reality of it struck me.

The next day I continued painting, not wanting to think about th significance, if indeed there was one.

Pater rarely took a day off work. He conscientiously took on h responsibility as the breadwinner. He lived within his means. We ha the same temperament, keeping to ourselves, preferring the compa of one or two others. It was from him that I took responsibility f

›ing the breadwinner. I always had a job teaching although I would uch rather have painted full time like artist friends.

Every now and then, after Mother died, it occurred to me that I iould visit my father. I always found excuses—a painting to finish, ı exhibition to prepare, a lecture to write. I knew that Lindsay had oked after our parents, helping them financially. I am ashamed to say ıat I allowed him to believe that my dedication to painting exempted e from keeping in touch with our parents. I never subscribed to the ›lief that an artist is granted a licence to ignore the rules that other ıman beings are obliged to follow.

T: You are appreciative of Lindsay and angry with your father.

When Mother protested about my decision to be an artist, Pater ›uld have said, 'Let the lad do what he wants.'

'he poet W.S. Merwin wrote a poem about the last time a man saw his ıther. The man didn't see his parents very often although they lived ı the same city. The last time he saw his father, the father was asking ›out his life. The father tells the son he wants him to stay and talk › him. The father goes into the next room to get something to give is son but as he does so he notices the son looking at his watch. The ıther says that he doesn't want the son to feel like he has to stay if he as important work to do or someone to see, 'I don't want to keep you'. he son leaves but there is nothing he has to do and no one he has to ›e. That was the last time he saw his father.

I imagine that Dad's father may have been like the father in the ›em, a father intimidated by his son, by his cleverness, by his status ı the world.

e says to T:

It crossed my mind to see Pater after Mother died. I imagined my ıther would see me as a man who had made it in a way he had not ıade it himself. I felt that my presence would unnerve him. I didn't want to embarrass him. As I said, I felt atavistic guilt for making s much more money than my father.

On Helen's instructions I went to my father's funeral. 'You cann not go to your father's funeral,' she said. She offered to come with m but I said I would rather get the whole thing over and done with alon In her absence she gave me instructions. 'You have to talk to peop You have to ask them who they are and how they know Mr Brac I asked a woman who she was. 'I'm your aunt.' After that I wasn listening to Lindsay's eulogy. I was planning my escape.

T: This was an opportunity to think about what your father mear to you, to pay your respects. It was an opportunity to sit and listen t the eulogy. It wouldn't matter if you didn't talk to anybody.

I was obediently doing what Helen had told me to do.

I want him to find compassion for his father.

He says to T:

I never told Lindsay that I was grateful to him for looking after ou parents, for helping them financially.

T: Unlike your brother, you carry the burden of remorse.

The next session he says to T:

This morning I stared at myself in the mirror, shaving. I saw m father's eyes, or what I remembered were his eyes. I realised I was th same age as my father when he died. I held the razor up to my chee put it down and then looked again in the mirror. A streak of bloo marked the place where the razor had pierced me. The thought cam to me: I am the same flesh and blood as my father.

In a novel by William Maxwell, the protagonist's mother dies in the fl epidemic of 1918. Many years later, after six months on the analyst' couch, he relives the night he paced with his arm around his father' 'aist, walking from room to room, stopping where his mother lay in er coffin. Together they stood looking at her. He meant to say to the nalyst, 'I couldn't bear it,' but what came out of his mouth was, 'I can't ear it.' Then Maxwell writes, 'This statement was followed by a flood f tears such as I hadn't known before, not even in my childhood.' He ets up and goes out into the New York street, 'a place where one can 'eep on the sidewalk in perfect privacy.'

[e tells T:

After the last session, I stepped outside onto the footpath, and as I id so, I remembered my father's words that day we returned from the ountry, 'It's nice to have the concrete under the feet.' Then I imagined, r thought I saw, a huge fissure open up in the concrete. I found myself ncontrollably sobbing in a flood of tears such as I had never known efore, not even in my childhood.

Today I stopped in the place where the fissure had opened up like a hasm. I picked up one of the magnolia petals that were covering the avement like a carpet. I examined the single petal as closely as I had xamined my face looking in the mirror shaving. The petal was pure vhite on one side and wine-red on the other. I scooped up a handful, eld them for a few moments and then let them fall in a little shower nto the concrete under my feet.

T: You are finding compassion for your father.

Silence.

T: If your heart can open for your father, could it also open for your nother? You do have the capacity to reconsider what you did in the ast. You told me that you later regretted taking the position you did n *Collins Street 5pm*.

When I was first asked to give lectures on art, I remember telling he audience, 'My mother didn't want me to be an artist. She said it vas just painting women with no clothes on.' I was ridiculing Mother for not knowing that the artist's model was referred to as 'the nu figure'. I knew I could get a laugh. Later I regretted it.

T: In mocking your mother for her ignorance you had demean yourself.

That's right. I can understand why Mother pushed us to do ve well at school, why she wanted us to have jobs where we would ea a decent salary. My parents could understand what Lindsay did as engineer but they saw no importance to the world in painting pictur They weren't interested in something as frivolous or grandiose as 't human condition'. They were concerned with how their sons cou make enough money to live on. I don't blame them for that.

It is not only working-class parents who have ambitions for their so Near the beginning of Patrick White's novel *The Twyborn Affair*, t father, a judge, asks his son, '"What do you think of doing, Eddie?" Y could hardly answer, Nothing; surely being is enough? looking, sm ing, listening, touching. Instead you said, "I'm thinking of going in the country. To work."'

The father offers to get his son a job in a firm of solicitors wi someone he knows. 'I'd die so much happier for seeing you dedicat to the Law.'

At the end of the novel Eddie has not entered the Law making h father happy. He is running a brothel and lives as a woman. 'He', nc 'she', is sitting on a park bench when she sees someone coming towar her. It is her mother with whom she has had a torturous relationsh The women sit side by side until the mother rummages in her handb takes out a pencil and writes on the fly leaf of a prayer book. 'Are yc my son Eddie?'

'No, but I am your daughter Eadith,' the other writes in response.

After a short pause, the mother says, 'I am so glad. I've alwa wanted a daughter.'

: says to T:

Mother wanted me to be a general in the army. My magnum opus as a painting of the Battle of Waterloo. I wasn't a general, but I had vested myself in a battle.

vant my father to reconcile with his mother. In a poem 'The Visitor', ary Oliver writes how on a moonless night she hears a frantic knockg on the door. She knows it is her father who has returned from the ad to pay her a visit. For a long time she doesn't open the door but entually the door opens of itself and she knows that she can bear nat she previously found repellent in her father.

If Mary Oliver could do that, I could get my father to do that.

: tells T:

Some days in the early evening I heard a knocking on the door. For e first few days it was a wild furious knock, then a short sharp smack d then a gentle, persistent tapping. I knew who was knocking, but as not yet ready to open the door and face what I knew I must face.

After four days I got up from my chair and walked towards the door nich opened by itself as I reached it. Mother was standing in the orway. I was about to say, 'What do you want?' but I said nothing. new what she wanted.

We looked each other eye to eye. She had aged in the forty years nce I had last seen her and yet she was indisputably my mother. ne made a move to step over the threshold into the house. I offered resistance. She sat down with the ease of one who had been here fore while I continued standing, not quite knowing what to do with yself. I was aware of the point of contention between us: my paintgs on the walls. As she focused her eyes on me, I heard myself saying, 'ould you like a cup of tea?'

'Yes, please, I'd love one,' she said. The sound of her voice took me ck to my childhood when I was the 'one' that she loved. I left her alone while I went into the kitchen to make the cup of tea. A shudd of nervous anticipation rushed through me, but I could not allow it get the better of me. It was years since I had made a cup of tea so I ha to concentrate on the procedure. I put the kettle on the stove. I four the teapot Helen used. I found a crumpled box of tea leaves and p three spoons of tea into the pot. I gathered two cups and saucers ar put them on a tray. I remembered to get the milk from the fridge. Th thought came to me, 'Mother might like a biscuit.' I seemed to reme ber that she was partial to a biscuit with a cup of tea. I looked in th cupboard and found the biscuit tin Helen always used. I opened th tin. I did not recall having seen these biscuits before. They were n the sort Helen would eat and I never eat biscuits myself. One side each biscuit was coated with pink or yellow icing and on the other sic the raised image of a clock face. I wondered whether I should taste or to check if they were palatable, but as I am no connoisseur I place them onto a saucer thinking that if Mother didn't like the look of the she didn't have to take one.

I brought the tea tray into the room where Mother was sitting b there was nowhere to put it. I placed it on the floor while I moved th book I was reading from the coffee table. I picked up the tray ar placed it onto the table, aware of my clumsiness as Mother sat sedate As I did this, Mother remarked, 'I see that you still like reading. Yo always had your nose in a book, I remember.'

'Yes, I still like reading,' I said, grateful for her small talk. I assume she had glanced at my pictures on the walls while I was making the te If she had, she kept her thoughts to herself. I poured the tea, trying n to fumble, and as I handed her the cup, the thought came to me, 'Th woman is my mother' as one might hold up one's hand and thir 'This is my hand,' fascinated that such a thing 'belonged' to oneself.

I poured myself some tea and offered the plate of biscuits. Moth took one with the pink icing, turned it over and said approving 'Tic Tocs.' I realised she was announcing the name of the biscuit, th c toc' referring to the clock face. She dunked the biscuit into the tea, olding it there for a few seconds, then took it out and raised it to her outh and took a bite. I pictured the clock face dissolving in the hot a as if time itself had dissolved between the present and the past. other's smile took me back to that memory of her praise and I found yself recalling what I saw and felt and knew when I was a little boy, vash with her loving attention to me.

In that moment, sitting in companionable silence with Mother, remember feeling, 'This is marvellous,' as one thinks looking at a embrandt self-portrait for the first time. I picked up one of the Tic Tocs ith the yellow icing, dunked it into the hot tea as Mother had done, eld it there for a few seconds, put it into my mouth and swallowed it. y thawed self was never more fully alive than in that moment sitting ith Mother after our long estrangement.

Mother said, 'I remember when Lindsay was a baby and you were vo years old. My whole day was spent looking after you and Lindsay, oing the washing, the cooking, the ironing, the cleaning. I remember nging for the day when I would sit down and you would give me a ıp of tea with a biscuit to nibble on.'

Mother had got what she longed for: the day when her first-born on would sit down and give her a cup of tea with a biscuit.

T: Sitting with your mother and having a cup of tea is one of your reatest achievements. Your mother got the cup of tea and a biscuit ıe had always wanted. What about you? Did you get what you ways wanted?

Mother must have seen the paintings on the walls. In ignoring ıem she was saying she accepted me as I am. I did not need her to nderstand the paintings. I did not need her approval. This is what felt was 'marvellous'. She had turned up. She had knocked on the oor and she had accepted me for who I am.

*

In the next session he says to T:

I remember a teacher saying, 'You must make your mind a goo companion because you live with it every minute of your life.' I had n friend. The teacher was telling me it was legitimate to make one's ow mind a companion.

T: Have you done what the teacher advised? Have you made you mind a good companion?

It's certainly a better companion than it was. In fact, I think it is good enough companion for us to end these sessions.

Last week, as I walked past the drycleaner's shop, I noticed se eral paintings of baby Jesus attached to the window. I stopped an looked. A sign said that they were painted by children from Grade 4 at St Mary's primary school. A nativity scene made of plasticine ha been constructed by the children of 5A. Mary's head had fallen t the side and one of the donkeys had nearly collapsed as two of hi legs could not support the weight of his plasticine body. I heard you words, 'There you are, finding fault, criticising other people's effort At that moment I became aware of my reflection in the window: an ol dishevelled man. I became aware of another reflection looking in th window and my thoughts were interrupted by a woman's voice.

'My son Dominic painted some of that picture.'

Then I heard myself saying, 'So this must be his first exhibition. It' a lovely painting.'

T: You could find generosity within yourself.

As I told you, I have done what the teacher said. I have made m mind a good companion.

T: What are you going to do now?

I am going to do a painting of the window of a drycleaning shop. I will show the children's paintings of the three wise men attached t the window with a sign saying *By St Mary's Grade 4B and 5A*. It wi show a plasticine nativity scene. In the background you will see a ma standing near the rows of drycleaned coats and jackets in their plasti ags. The pièce de résistance will be my reflection outside the window, ›oking in. It will be my final self-portrait.

I once did a painting of a shop window of surgical equipment. rutches dangled from a hook. At the bottom of the window, several ʼalking sticks were displayed higgledy-piggledy with a sign saying, . walking stick makes a good companion.' The teacher said, 'We must ıake our mind a good companion.' If I had dementia, I would have no ıind at all. I would have lost my mind. I would have no companion. ou have been my walking stick, my good companion.

T: I have been your walking stick and now you have found the apacity to walk alone.

They are both silent for a while as if pretending to be listening to ıe rain.

T: Our time is up, all our time is up, this is the end of our work ›gether.

Thank you. Thank you from the bottom of my heart.

They shake hands.

He walks out into the street and then enters a shop and buys an :e-cream. He sits on a seat near a playground watching the children laying. A ball lands near his feet. He picks it up and throws it back to he children and then he resumes eating the ice-cream.

Whether or not it is the grace of God, I like to think that it was grace hat my father found when he sat on the seat eating the ice-cream, hrowing the ball back to the children playing.

'Each of us has a public life and a private life. But beyond both is a secret life that baffles us.'

Richard Flanagan, *Question 7*

My Mother

My mother *had* found grace. She tells me how she was walking alo a busy street when it started to rain. As she walked, she put one ar into the sleeve of her raincoat and was grappling with the other slee dangling behind her back when a hand appeared from behind, guidi her arm into the sleeve. The Guider-of-the-Arm continued walki disappearing into the crowd, leaving my mother's thanks dangli with no one to receive them. 'Do you know what that was?' she sa 'That was the Grace of God.'

She does not see it as the kindness of strangers.

We were having lunch, our plates balanced on our knees. Our cu of tea perched precariously on papers covering a small coffee tab Nietzsche's *Being and Nothingness* peeped out from beneath a conce program partially covered by a bank statement, a glossy brochu for a gallery event jostled with the train timetable, a message to 'th householder', a postcard 'Dear Helen'. A single piece of paper in m mother's distinctive handwriting floated on the top. It read like th titles of her paintings.

The true but hidden self that is veiled by the flesh.
Everyday feelings of Guilt. The yearning for Redemption
for the blessing that relieves us of our Guilt.

My mother had not invited me to read what she had written b neither had she covered it up.

I wondered aloud about a man on trial for the deaths of an elderly uple whose bodies he burnt into smithereens. 'For the rest of his e he has to live with the guilt of what he did to their bodies,' I said. nderstandably, my mother did not take my oblique reference to the ilt of another to speak about her own.

She had given other clues for what she was seeking. For a time, she ould excitedly ask at family gatherings, 'Have you seen the televi-on series *Queen Victoria*? There's a simply divine Lord Melbourne. e would all love a Lord Melbourne.' Curious to know her fascination ith Lord Melbourne, I watched the television series.

At eighteen, Victoria becomes queen, consulting with the Prime inister, Lord Melbourne, a man old enough to be her father. He lvises her, coming when she calls him, guiding her, listening, end-ssly patient, never ridiculing her for her ignorance about matters of e state. The beautiful young Queen Victoria falls in love with the arismatic Lord Melbourne who very properly does not surrender either his or her desires. In my mother's hankering after her own ord Melbourne, I saw her as yearning for a father who had the time be there for her, guiding her, coming when she called him, listening her worries.

When my mother was growing up, she did not see her father except say good morning and good night. 'I told you, Dad left for work at ven-thirty in the morning and came home at seven at night.' The ildren were brought up by nannies. They had meals with Nanny in e nursery. On the weekends, their father saw his patients, went to is club and played golf. On holidays he drove them to a guesthouse here he left them in the care of Nanny.

For years I could not reach my father. On family occasions I asked im questions about art. Wanting something more but not knowing ow to get it, I figured out that as he communicated to me in his paint-gs, I would respond to him in my form of painting. I devised a letter ith photographs, binding it in the form of a book, telling him not to look at it until I had left to go home. Ten minutes after arriving home the phone rang. It was Mum.

'John was so pleased with your book.'

A silence followed and then the clattering of her phone dropping and then: 'I wish my father had seen my paintings and understood them.'

In all the years of my mother's exhibition openings, I never saw her father or her mother. They would have received an invitation. She must have wondered why they weren't there.

I saw my father in his paintings. My mother did not see her father in his very private work, and in not coming to her exhibitions, he did not see her in hers. The title of a painting, painted in her nineties: *The desire to relate to a Superior Other but Not Seen by him*. A few years later: *There is no Feedback so is What I do Worthwhile? Self Doubt*.

As I saw it, my mother was giving clues about her deepest needs in her note left on the table, in her fascination with the television program, in the titles of her paintings. She was telling us her desire to be seen by a 'superior other', the desire for feedback on her work, for a father figure who had the time to show his love for her, who had seen her paintings and understood them, another human being who could offer redemption from her guilt.

The therapist had listened to my father. I was curious to know what would happen if a therapist listened to my mother. She would not actively seek out a therapist; she expressed her inner life in her paintings. She referred to 'that psychoanalytic stuff' as 'hopeless' as it applied to her painting and yet she read books by the psychoanalyst Adam Phillips. In a chapter 'On Not Getting It', she had written *too stupid* in the margins. She referred to those who did not 'get' her paintings as 'too stupid' to get them. In *Art as Therapy* she shouted into the margins: *YES!!! Not so!!!!! Art isn't about 'beauty'. Purpose of art Self knowledge!?* She tells me she is reading a marvellous book on Hitler's childhood, hoping to discover why he did the evil things that he did.

It was not until after her death that she gave herself permission to tell the world her deepest troubles. In a fifteen-page speech to be read at her funeral, she revealed her thoughts about her painting, her relationship to Dad, her views on the art world, her private agonies and misgivings.

She knew from experience and humiliation that the seven deadly sins applied to her, to be navigated, and she knew from experience how distorting each deadly sin is when it dominates…She regretted her savagery to others, whilst condemning those who savaged her.

The speech to be read publicly at her funeral seemed more suited to the privacy of the consulting room of the therapist than the exposure of the public gathering of family, friends, artists and gallery directors. It read as a vindication to the art world, an appeal to be understood, an appeal to be absolved of her misgivings.

I had intended to create a scenario where my mother visits a therapist as my father had with T. At ninety-seven she would not consider seeing a therapist but I can imagine that she would respond to a stranger who would listen to her kindly. I will arrange for her to meet such a person. He will have the skills and experience of a chaplain, a doula, a spiritual advisor. He will have worked as a psychiatrist and in his retirement will have been called upon to hold the hands of those who are dying. His work as a psychiatrist will give him legitimacy in my mother's eyes. It will have given him the awareness of how we are shaped by our childhoods, the power of the unconscious, how we say one thing and mean another. He will have listened to stories of those who had never spoken of the child they were forced to give up for adoption, of those haunted by guilt of the crime they got away with, of those who had kept their sexuality hidden. He will offer not only what my mother experienced from the man who had helped her put her arm into the sleeve of her raincoat, but the opportunity to unburden herself of what troubles her and for which she is seeking atonement.

Given that she would not seek out the man I refer to as V, I w invent a scenario where he would find himself offering his comp ionship to her.

Mum sometimes received requests for information about h father as president of the Melbourne Club and his role in the forn tion of the Royal College of Psychiatrists. V will contact her to a about her father as a member of the Melbourne Establishment. I will send a driver to collect her and bring her to his house not far fro her childhood home. He will have the manners, the charm and t self-confidence of a man who was brought up with a sense of entit ment and who elicits respect from this entitlement. My mother w defer to this man who will remind her of her father. She will tell hi of her grandfather Sir Henry Carr Maudsley who was knighted for h services in the First World War, and who was said to have occupi an exalted place in the history of Australian medicine. She will t of her grandmother Lady Maudsley, daughter of Canon Stretch, w took a leading part in the social and artistic life of Melbourne. She w tell how, aged three, she had been ticked off by Lady Maudsley f slurping the butter out of a scone and how her grandfather had sub quently copied what she did, winking at her. She will tell of what s knows of her father's role in the First and Second World Wars and his medical achievements.

Sessions with V

She says to V:

Dad was a darling man, so charming and conscientious, so ha working. He didn't have it all easy. He was born with a cleft pala The other boys at Melbourne Grammar teased him for his lisp. H figured out that to be accepted, he had to become very good at spo And so he did. He trained very hard and won medals for his school. W hardly saw him, he was so busy at work. I remember when he call my sisters and me together. 'Look what I've got Mummy for her birt day.' He unwrapped a parcel. 'It's a lace tablecloth,' he said. 'Mumm will love it.'

The next day we eagerly watched as Mum unwrapped the birthd present he had bought. 'Take that back,' she said, tossing it aside. Sh had recognised the lace as the same lace as a doily that one of Dad patients had made for him and given him not long after their fir meeting.

V: It was then that you learnt that despite his considerable achiev ments, like all of us, your father had his flaws.

The reference to her father's flaws immediately summons up h own. She tells V what she told a family gathering in a speech on h ninetieth birthday.

It's all the things I did wrong that I remember. And then I think, nust have got something right, but perhaps I didn't.

V: You are asking for confirmation that you got 'something right'.

I am sure I did get something right. I am not a total and utter failure.

V: No, you definitely are not.

I really could have done better given my advantages.

V: You are very hard on yourself.

My work wasn't even mentioned in a major book on the history of ustralian art. John's work was mentioned but nothing about mine. s if I didn't exist. Sometimes I wonder whether all my work will just) into the rubbish bin for all the interest that is shown.

V: It is very disappointing to you, very hurtful, to be excluded. At ıe end of your life, you are seeking some sign that your work has ɛen worthwhile, that you yourself are worthwhile. Let us continue ıese conversations once a week.

Mum's work was not given the acclaim that was given to Dad's ork. It is not as accessible, it is complex, not easily identifiable.

Unexpectedly, I once came upon a postcard of one of her early aintings in the gallery shop of the National Gallery of Victoria. It epicted a curved backbone with two white hexagon shapes at the p. A green wreath was clasped around the hips. Two lobster legs rotruded, bent at the knees, their claw pincers dangling, supposedly ıe feet. In not preparing myself to see my mother's paintings as I did hen I went to her exhibitions, I glimpsed how others might see them or the first time.

There was something disconcerting about the image, something lmost repellent, cold and elusive. The image on the postcard was ot pure abstract; neither was it purely realistic. The flesh had been rained from the body.

I turned the postcard over to read the title. *The Listening Lady*, 1956. title leads us into the painting. This title confused me. What tells us the lady is listening? Despite the skill of the painting and the subtl beauty of the muted tones, I imagined that the postcards would be le there, discarded, as if saying, 'No one wants one of us.'

I found myself wishing to defend the painting against the criticis I myself was making. It was my mother's painting. I knew how har she worked.

Something further unsettled me. On the back of the postcard nex to the title I read, *Gift of the artist*. 'That's kind,' I thought, 'a gif I recalled Mum saying, 'I've given one of John's paintings to the galler the NGV. That's where his work will be most appreciated. I've include several paintings of my own.' For years, Mum was disappointed tha the NGV had not bought one of her significant later works and rarel displayed the few early ones in its collection. She would rather th gallery bought a painting but since they had not, she had given severa as a gift in a package they could not refuse. My admiration for he ingenuity in getting her painting into the gallery collection was ove shadowed by the humiliation at the need to give such a gift.

A few days later, I came across a short item in the newspape '*Two Running Girls*, a John Brack oil on board, was sold at auction fo $1.65m.' In 1959, when my father was painting *Two Running Girls*, m mother was cooking the meals for my father and the four of us girl She was sewing and knitting most of the clothes and doing all th housework as well as doing her own painting and tending to the need of the man who painted *Two Running Girls*.

His painting was sold for over one million dollars.

Her painting was given as a gift in a package of his paintings.

*

In the next session she says to V:

Every so often I wake up in the night with everyday feelings o guilt, yearning for the blessing that relieves us of our guilt.

V: Tell me about guilt.

Well, just everyday feelings of guilt. If I don't go for a walk, I feel uilt. If someone points out a mistake, I feel guilt. If I don't write the cceptance letter straight away, I feel guilt. Guilt about the murderous ıoughts about John. Guilt about not being worthwhile. Guilt about ıy failings with the children.

V: Your guilt overwhelms you. You cannot let it go.

In noting the date of her marriage on my birth certificate and the ate of my birth, I assume that she had to get married.

She tells V:

I remember the terrible guilt when I discovered that I was pregnant. knew we would have to get married.

V: Instead of feeling joy that you were expecting a baby, giving our mother a grandchild, you were overcome with guilt.

Well, I hadn't planned to get pregnant. It was my fault. I also knew hat I was disappointing Mum in not marrying some gorgeous young ıan, the son of a friend, a young man who was training to be a doctor, lawyer, a diplomat. Here I was, marrying an artist from a family my arents had never even heard of. I was more determined than ever to rove that John could be successful as an artist, to prove that John as not a nobody.

*

n the next session she arrives with wet hair. She has walked from he car to V's room, not permitting the driver to accompany her with n umbrella.

V: Oh dear, I see you have been caught in the rain Helen. Would you ike to lie down on the couch? Let me put a blanket over you.

I'm not an invalid, you know.

V: I know you are not an invalid. I just want to make you comfc able and warm. You can talk to me lying on the couch.

No no no. I would rather sit on the chair.

After a silence she says: As a child I *was* an invalid for one ye I was having fun with other children running and jumping from t sand dunes when I landed on a stick. It was excruciatingly painf The pain of the walk from the sand dunes to the guesthouse whe we were staying was like nothing I had ever experienced before. T stick had embedded itself into my foot so deeply you could not s any evidence of it. The foot felt terribly painful even after the sti was removed. No one believed me. How could the stick still be causi pain when it had been taken out? Later it was discovered that I h osteomyelitis caused by an infection from the stick.

V: That sounds traumatic.

Well, I don't know about 'traumatic'. I just remember the excru ating pain.

V: And initially no one believed you.

Often Mum feels that she is not believed, not heard, not understoo Dad did not believe her when she told him that Seurat was using t same technique they were being taught but when she showed hi the book, 'he had to admit I was right'. She did a series of paintin on the theme of Cassandra after the mythical figure no one believed

Mum had told V about the stick in her foot in their first meetin There is another event in her life that I imagine she would tell someo who was prepared to listen.

She tells V:

About thirty years after my mother died, I got a phone call from cousin I hardly knew. As we chatted about our childhoods, the cous mentioned our common grandmother. I told her that she was mistak our grandmother had died before I was born. It seemed that the cous

.d received letters and cards, Christmas and birthday presents, oney for pony-riding lessons.

After I put down the phone, I looked up the Public Records Office ıere I discovered that Grace McCall died in Melbourne in 1946. At e time of her death, I was nineteen. The place of her death was not r from where I lived all my childhood.

V: Your parents had betrayed you.

It was the shock of it. I could not understand why our grandmother as kept hidden from the grandchildren who lived in the same city ıt not those who lived overseas. I wondered if she was mad or an coholic or had some horrible disfigurement.

I discovered that Grace McCall worked as a housekeeper for a Laing. Dr Laing's daughter Nancy was a frequent visitor to our ouse. It could be that she was not just a housekeeper, she was living the de facto wife of Dr Laing.

If it was known that Hal Maudsley's mother-in-law was living 'in n', the reputation of the Maudsley family would have been damed. As you know, Dad was president of the Melbourne Club and was his father before that. They were very important members of e Melbourne Establishment, a close-knit group of doctors, lawyers, dges and politicians. If someone was in trouble with the law, a wyer friend could oblige. If a daughter needed an abortion, illegal the time, a medical friend could perform the operation. If the fees r the private school could not be paid, assistance was discreetly ovided.

V: So, whatever the reason Grace McCall was hidden, it was beyond e expertise, the influence or the strings that could be pulled by the elbourne Establishment.

It had to be kept from the Melbourne Establishment. A divorce, a iving offence or some other misdemeanour from a reputable family ould be reported in the newspaper as a scandal.

Once, when sensing Mum's anger with her mother for keeping h grandmother a secret, I took the risk of asking her the question. 'Ho do you feel about your mother for keeping her own mother hidden?'

After a long silence she coldly replied, 'I never know what peop mean when they ask me questions like that.'

She says to V:

There were other secrets to be kept in the family, things that we no one else's business. Dad was addicted to the morphine that he ha for injuries in the war. It was a terrible, terrible ordeal for Mum g ting him off the addiction. I remember all the whisperings and silen in those times of withdrawal.

V: You had to keep this a secret in the family.

Mum could get Dad off his addiction, but I could not get John off h

V: Unlike your mother, you felt that you had failed.

I remember the doctor telling me that John's dementia was th result of his drinking. Nobody had told me he was an alcoholic. Th beautiful brain going down the gurgler. If I had known John was a alcoholic, I would have done something to prevent it. I *did* do som thing. More than once, I poured the bottle of whiskey down the sir thinking it may as well go down the plughole as into John's stomach

V: Perhaps you knew there was nothing you could do to stop John drinking.

I should have known that he was drinking too much. I should hav known that his drinking would cause brain damage. It was stup of me not to know. I remember being struck by the lovely Germa woman who managed the guesthouse where I was staying in Berli She said to me the first morning at breakfast, 'You know, we had n idea what was going on during the war. We knew nothing about it. W were as shocked as anyone when we found out.'

V: You are telling me that we can know something but also keep it secret from ourselves.

I remember hearing cries like a wild animal in the night. It was ter-fying. I didn't know what it was until Mum told me it was Dad calling ıt in dreams. In the First World War he was straight out of medical :hool, a medical officer in the Field Ambulance, the first on the scene 'ter battle. Nothing in his medical training could have prepared him r what he experienced in the war. He did not talk about it although ere were little glimpses in the diaries he had written.

V: Publicly your father was applauded for his bravery in the war. ivately he suffered the trauma of the war.

As a psychiatrist he gave shock treatment to those who had suffered hat was known as shellshock. I understand it was very effective.

The psychoanalyst Nicolas Abraham refers to the 'dead who…took nspeakable secrets to the grave'. While the secret itself goes to the ave, the knowledge of a secret 'haunts' the living. The 'concealment some part of a loved one's life' produces 'a gap' in the children and andchildren. 'What haunts are not the dead, but the gaps left within s by the secrets of others.'

For years Mum made repeated references to the 'feral', speaking ith revulsion of what humans do to each other. I assumed her ference to the feral arose from her disgust with the feral within er. Now I wonder whether it refers to the haunting of her father and er grandfather. Many of her paintings depict the symbols of war, oating shards, disembodied remnants, fragments. The titles of the aintings:

> *Our Civilised Minds, Our Feral Mindlessness, Our Inherited Language; our Re-configuration. The Hyena Laugh,* 2013.
>
> *Not 'The Civilized and the Barbaric'. But, 'The Civilized and the Feral'*, 2013.

Perhaps the haunting passed on from her father and her grand-ther found expression in the images and the titles of the paintings.

In response to Mum's comments about the trauma of her father i the First World War, V says: Your father took unspeakable secrets t the grave. You are haunted by what you do not know of those secret You are experiencing what we now refer to as 'intergeneration trauma', the trauma passed on from one generation to the next.

I don't know. That just sounds like poppycock to me.

I do not know my mother's experience of the haunting. The stoicis of her class and generation meant that one battled on with littl sympathy for those who drew attention to a discomfort, let alone trauma they could not explain. The titles of two paintings, twenty year apart:

Not Safe to Reveal, Held in the Darkness, 2004.
Knowingly Hidden; Covered, Not Seen Not Revealed, 2024.

I do not know the secrets my mother carried from her childhood, bu I *do* know her response to me telling her a secret from my childhood.

I was ten years old, walking home after playing at a friend's hous after school. A man approached me. He told me he was lost. He aske me where [name of street] was. I cannot explain what led me to follo the man. I had been put under a spell. He spoke to me kindly. I wa obediently doing what he asked of me.

When we reached the creek, I lay down by the creek bed as the ma asked. I had no will. The man did what I later understood was rap I cannot remember any pain. I cannot remember fear. I was lookin down from above, observing myself.

For months I lay in bed at night imagining the headmaster callin me to the front of the whole school on Monday morning assembl pointing to me, saying 'This girl is pregnant.' I did not know wha had prompted this fantasy as no child had ever been called up an ridiculed in front of the school. I know now that this was the sham of the rape.

The shame was compounded by the guilt that I should tell my other. I could not imagine telling her. It would be my fault. She would sk me why I had disobeyed her, talking to a stranger. She had enough orries looking after my father and three younger children. I had no nguage to describe what the man had done to me. As a ten-year-old could spell 'camouflage' and 'deciduous trees' but I had never come cross the words 'vagina', 'penis' or 'rape'.

In my early thirties I wrote a letter telling my mother what had appened at the creek bed. I wanted her to know. The burden of the ecret was now exacerbated by the burden of the writing, which I oped would release me from the secret. After so long in hiding I could ot burst out spontaneously describing what had happened. I had consider how to tell my mother, how to prepare her for what no other would want to hear.

After more than six months I dropped the letter into the letterbox. hree days later I opened the front door to see my mother holding a lant wrapped in cellophane and done up with a ribbon. 'It's a...' she aid, naming the plant. 'I bought it from a nursery on the way here. It kes shade.'

I took this gift on the unexpected visit as my mother's way of saying he had read the letter. I invited her in and put the kettle on the stove.

'I wonder if that happened to Vicky. One day she came home from chool covered in bruises.' Mum wondered aloud about Vicky until had composed myself sufficiently to suggest going outside to plant he shrub she had bought. My two young daughters assisted with the lanting, innocent of the meaning of it. My mother had not responded s I feared she would if I had told her when it happened. She did not nply that it was my fault. It would not be characteristic of her to armly give me a hug and say, 'I'm so sorry.' It surprised me that I was ot more upset by her reaction and yet it confirmed why I had not told er when it happened.

In not telling my mother before then, I had wanted to protect h She had so many worries. One more worry could undo her. As t eldest child, I knew that it was up to me to help look after the young children, to make things easier for Mum, not to be any 'trouble', not make any additional demands on her. If she fell apart, who would lo after us? Who would look after Daddy?

Mum tells me, 'You were about two years old. I was sewing. Y were playing. It was raining. Suddenly there was a crash of thund and then lightning, and then I looked up to see you running into t room holding the baby, the baby's head narrowly missing the doorwa

I do not remember carrying the baby, but I do remember slippi the holiday pocket money from my grandmother into my mothe purse.

At the time I posted the letter about the rape, I did not have to prote my mother anymore. My responsibilities were to my children. I w free of the secret, but I had given my mother the burden of knowing the rape. As far as I know, there was no one she could talk to about i

Twenty years after sending the letter, the proceedings of the roy commission into institutional responses to child sexual abuse we reported in the newspapers. I asked Mum if she had been followi the news.

'Yes, I have. It's terrible. It's truly terrible what happened to tho children. I cannot bear thinking about it.'

'Yes, it's awful,' I said. 'Imagine being sexually abused by someo in authority, someone you trusted, someone your parents trusted, teacher, a Catholic priest.'

'It's too awful to think about,' my mother said.

'It takes courage to tell what happened, especially publicly in royal commission.'

'Yes,' my mother agreed, and then, looking vacantly into the d tance as if not speaking to me, she said, 'Some people can't even t their mothers, you know.'

'Yes, I *do* know,' I replied.

My mother was telling *me* that *some people* could not tell *their* ɔthers.

'It's not just the abuse that's so damaging,' I said. 'It's the secrecy of the years of keeping the secret.'

On the way home I wondered if Mum remembered the letter. After e visit with the plant, the rape had never been referred to again.

A few weeks later, we were talking about the funny things little ildren say. Mum said, 'John was walking over the bridge at the creek the bottom of the hill. A little girl ran up to him saying, "Are you a ranger?"'

It was uncanny. That was the bridge I saw from my vantage point ing face down on the creek bed as the man raped me.

After telling my therapist about the rape, I realised that I needed meone to tell me it was a violation. I needed someone to tell me that wasn't my fault.

I do not know what secrets my mother is carrying but I want her have the release from the burden of keeping the secret, despite not owing what the secret is or indeed whether there is one.

How would I get my mother to tell V the secret she is carrying?

At age eleven she was in bed for one year with osteomyelitis, in e care of a nurse in a huge Victorian mansion. An odd-job man ɔuld be chopping wood, a housekeeper mopping the floors, trades-en delivering things to the house. I picture the young girl wheeled ıt into the garden on a chaise longue, left there with her drawing d and pencils while the nurse returned to chores inside the house. ɔicture a gardener chatting to the young girl who could not walk, nfined to her chaise longue. I picture him bringing flowers for her draw, tearing one apart, his calloused hands tenderly gripping the amens and the petals, explaining the parts of the flower to her. I sist writing the hand reaching under the woollen tartan blanket, its ssels dangling onto the grass. Vaguely I picture the chaise longue capsizing with the body of the big man on top of the girl, one har over her mouth suppressing her scream, the pages of the sketches the parts of the flower loosened from the drawing pad, fluttering the newly manicured lawn.

I wondered what stopped me from the description of the act violation.

Perhaps I did not want to imagine that this had 'happened' my mother. Perhaps it was because I heard her saying, 'No, that didn happen.' Perhaps it was because I could not imagine my mother tellin another person. Perhaps my desire for my mother to tell the secr arose from my wish to be free of the haunting of what I did not kno and what I would never know.

I was disappointed not to have breathed life into this fiction scenario. I had wanted my mother to be free of the shame of the secr to be free of the burden of keeping a secret.

It was not only that. I wanted something from V. I wanted to crea a scenario where he would lovingly embrace my mother and say, 'I a so, so sorry.'

*

She says to V:

Mum was an enormous support for Dad. She didn't put up wi any nonsense. I once heard a colleague of Dad's describe her as 'som what terrifying', adding that she had 'a wonderfully kind heart'. Sh was an amazingly competent woman. She could have been a matro in a hospital. Her job was managing the household, doing volunte work and social activities required of Dad's work. That's what docto wives did in those days. She had a strong sense of noblesse oblig She was president of the Truby King League of Victoria; she did a l of work for Travellers' Aid. I didn't really see much of her except c Sunday afternoon and Nanny's day off.

V: So who looked after you in the absence of your mother?

We were looked after by nannies. I had become very fond of Nanny evens. One day she wasn't there. Replaced by another nanny. I dn't understand it. No one told me why she wasn't there and wasn't ming back. Later I wondered if she had left to get married. I waited r her to come but she never did.

V: The person you loved was taken away from you without any planation.

I thought it must have been my fault. I wondered if I had said mething to upset her.

V: There was no one to console you.

Well, you know, you just get on with life. What else is there to do?

V: I am wondering if you can feel for that little girl whose nanny she ved was taken away from her. I am wondering if you could consider e loss and bewilderment for that little girl.

She winces at what she would see as sentimentality and then says: was a long time in the past. You get over it.

V: It is difficult for you to hear what must have been painful for you a child. I am wondering if you could be sympathetic to your own ounded younger self.

That's just pathetic. I told you, you just get over it. That's just ibbish.

Mum was not given to expressions of sympathy or grief either r herself or for others. It appalled her that her mother had 'wailed for week' after the dog died. 'I mean, all about a dog. It's pathetic.' We ere discussing a book we had both read, the story of a woman who med a hawk as a way of working through her grief after the death f her father. 'I don't know why she had to go on and on about the ther. A grown-up woman going on about how she misses him. It's so dious. Why couldn't she just get over it? I mean, I ask you. It's just o silly for words.' She asked about my daughter who had postnatal depression. 'She's much better,' I said. 'Oh good, I am glad she's reco ered.' I was giving the answer she wanted to hear. Her question 'Ho are you?' was often followed with, 'If you're not all right, don't tell m I don't want to know.'

After V invites her to be sympathetic to her own wounded younge self, she doesn't turn up to the next session. She doesn't let V kno that she won't be coming.

When she returns, she says to V: Oh, so you are here?

V: You thought I might have given up on you, abandoned you lik Nanny Stevens.

No no no. I imagined that you were sitting looking out the windo wondering where I was.

*

At Mum's ninetieth birthday we had gathered for afternoon tea—fou children, ten grandchildren, two great-grandchildren and Mum' cousin Edward and his wife. At one point in the proceedings Mum sai she wanted to read a speech. Later she gave me a copy.

'It is fun to be ninety, more fun than eighty-nine.'

This seemed disingenuous. Mum considered 'fun' to be superficial

'Now for regrets. I regret that you have all done more for me tha I have for you. I regret that I wasn't kinder to people. I must have go something right but maybe I didn't.' She concluded by saying how proud she was of us all. The pride in us all felt as disingenuous as 'it i fun to be ninety'.

After half-hearted applause a silence followed. I knew what I wa expected to say but no words would come. No words would come fron anybody else until Edward, perhaps sensing that something neede to be said, remarked on the wonderful spread of cakes that had bee provided. This reminded Mum of a memory from her childhood.

'I was three years old. It was Easter. We had gone to visit Grandmother and Grandfather. I picked up a scone and slurped the butter out of the middle. Grandmother looked at me scowling, "Don't do that." Grandfather picked up a scone and copied what I did, winking at me.'

That's what she wanted, someone to wink at her, to acknowledge her, someone to say she had been a good mother, to say that she had got something 'right'.

In her vulnerability she says to V:

You have to remember that our family was based on the manners of the British upper class. Mum loved the Queen. When the Queen visited Melbourne in 1954 Mum went to great lengths to get us an invitation to the garden party. John would have hated it. Mum just assumed we would take up the invitation, furious when we didn't.

V: You had very different values from your mother and yet you carry the manners she instilled.

I was prohibited from eating any of the scrumptious-looking cakes at the ninetieth birthday as two days after I was scheduled for a bowel cancer operation. I told my friend Frances about my despondency at having failed my mother in not responding to her speech. She made a cup of tea and offered me a piece of orange cake she had made. As my eyes met the cake, I visualised the page of rules to follow before the operation. 'No food' and before that 'only white food, white rice, white chicken, white bread'. This was orange cake.

My hand reached out and picked up what was forbidden. I took one bite and then another. It felt like an act of defiance against my mother. 'No means no.' It was not only that. We had been sharing our feelings about our respective family gatherings. A piece of cake is the epitome of sharing.

Mum would reject the offer of 'sharing'. I could not think of a friend she could ring to tell of her disappointment at the response to her ninetieth birthday speech. She tried so hard to do or say the rig thing without questioning the wisdom of what she perceived as t right thing. How could you be wrong if you were so conscientiou Before giving a talk or opening an exhibition she would spend hou studying the paintings, taking notes, writing and revising her spee with a diligence that often seemed out of proportion to what w being asked of her. I remember once walking her back to her car wh her thoughts spoke themselves aloud, 'All that effort, but for wha Despite the applause, the thanks, the bouquet of flowers, somethi was missing. As she says in her funeral speech: 'If I had known wh was right, I would have done it.'

Perhaps if she had known love from her mother, if she had know the love of her grandmother, she would not have punished hers for what she saw as her failings. I have no doubt that her moth and father did love her, but they were not there for her. She berat herself, seeking affirmation that she did get something right b even if we reassured her—'You were a good enough mother'—I dou those words would have consoled her. Who were we? We were 'on her children.

*

She tells V:

From the age of five I was taught at home by a governess. I w very conscientious. When I turned eight, I started at St Catherine Instead of being in a class of three others, I was in a class of twen others. I hated it. In some lessons I was far ahead, seen as a know-a and in other lessons I was way behind, seen as a dunce. It was awf I could never figure out what the teacher expected from me. If I ha known what was right, I would have done it. At home I was expecte to do well at my schoolwork, but I was also expected to be social acceptable which meant not being serious about my work. When I g ler, I was expected to be glamorous but not too glamorous, clever t not too clever.

V: You had a lot to be bewildered about. Your nanny left with no planation. You were thrust into a class of twenty other children, in me subjects way ahead, in others way behind. You were expected to well at school but not too well. It is understandable that you would wary of trusting authority.

Long silence.

Twice in my life I did trust authority.

V: Tell me about it.

After I left the gallery school, I was very unsettled. I didn't know hat sort of artist I wanted to be. I knew that I *didn't* want to do real-ic painting, but I didn't know what sort of painting I *did* want to do. ien, by chance, I discovered the direction I would take.

Every day I sat opposite the same woman on the tram. I had never en anyone like her before. I couldn't say what fascinated me. I anted to draw her portrait, but I knew I could not sit opposite her etching from the model as we were trained to do at art school.

When I got home, I drew a sketch of her from memory, playing ith the image, stylising it, exaggerating shapes, moving bits around. ventually I'd got it. The drawing looked like her, but it was not like portrait. It wasn't like any other drawing I had ever seen. I didn't ıow if it was rubbish. I showed it to a respected art critic who said, ıat is the most erotic drawing I have ever seen.' It was one of the ost encouraging things anyone had ever said to me about my work. vas young and naïve. At nineteen I had never heard the word 'erotic'. was the 'erotic' that had fascinated me. It was the erotic that the awing depicted. For me this was my *Opus 1*.

V: The respected art critic gave you permission to continue this pproach to drawing.

He had shown me the direction to take. I had stylised the woman ith exaggerated shapes. Over the years the subjects became more and more stylised and pared back. Numbers, letters and disembodi objects float across the canvas: a pillar, a crown, a doorknob, a sh The paintings play with perspective. Depending on how you look it, a ladder is going up or down, the window is looking out or looki in. The Mobius strip, a three-dimensional figure eight, twirls back in itself, making the inside become the outside.

The titles were originally short—*The Journey, The Encounter, T Listening Lady*. But then, another man I respected suggested long titles. He suggested writing in the title what I had told him about t painting. From then on, I wrote longer titles and then even long When they became even longer I called the paintings 'visual essays'.

V: Your work has been very much in response to the advice these two men you respected. Their suggestions gave it legitimacy.

*

In 2017, an exhibition of Mum's work was held at the National Galle of Victoria with three other women artists. The critic Sasha Grish wrote that since first encountering her work, he was struck by 'i complexity, its quiet, reserved beauty and the intellectual engagemer As he says, 'The paintings do not leap off the walls crying for attentic but once you pause for a moment, look and enter the work, you a drawn into a visual and intellectual labyrinth of endless complexit He concludes by saying, 'Maudsley is not a difficult artist to appre ate, but there is a certain threshold to overcome before you can ent her intriguing and perplexing world.'

Standing at the threshold, some ask, 'What's the code?' Infuriat at being asked, Mum made this into the title of a painting, there showing us the origin of the titles.

She tells V:

As I said, the titles come from what I am thinking at the time of ɔing the painting. It infuriated me when people asked for the code— ‧ if there *was* a code—so I made that the title of the painting.

'I Want to be In It'; 'There's Nothing to be In On' 'What's the Code' 'There is no Code' 'This is Rubbish and you're not Getting Away ith It'

V: The title is a retaliation to those who didn't get their meaning.

They were too stupid to get it. Once my work had finally become ›tter known, I got the impression that young women artists thought ⸦new things I didn't. They thought I had a special trick of getting my ork into a gallery, of having articles written about my work. They ‧w that I had got something they wanted, and they were determined ‧ get it. When I told them that was rubbish, I couldn't tell them how to ›t it, they didn't want to know me. It's not as if your work is accepted .st by magic. It's not as if you can tell someone in a sentence, passing on so they can do it themselves. So then I made that the title of the ainting.

'You Know Something that I don't, and I Want it; I'm the
same as You'
'No you're Not. I haven't Got what you think I've Got.'
'Yes You Have and you wont let me Have it, but if I Match
you, I'll Get it.'
'When you find out I Haven't Got what you think I've Got. I
will be your Enemy.'
'If I don't Get it and Everyone else Does, I'll look Stupid, so
I Pretend to
Get it, but I'll Hate you. When No one Gets it, I'll join the
Pack and Kill you. If
you withstand this, You're Mad'

V: So that is the title of one painting?

As I said, they are visual essays.

V: The titles of the paintings are doing something with your ange

When my work was not included in a book on the history of Au tralian art, I painted several pictures, *The Power of The Written Wor Without the Written Word, Art doesn't Exist.*

V: The title reads as an invitation to write about your work.

She says nothing.

In the next session V asks:

I am wondering how the words of the title connect to the visu image of the painting.

Well, sometimes there are motifs in the picture connecting to th title—question marks, symbols, letters of the alphabet.

V: So the motifs or symbols are there to be deciphered in referenc to the words of the title.

Well, you know the title means what it says because I say it. It's lik the mother saying to the child, 'No means no.'

When Emily was little, sometimes I was asked to keep an eye on he to see that she didn't get into mischief. It was then that I discovere that two-year-old Emily had a will of her own and was not the exte sion of a doll. I have never forgotten it. I could not get her to obey m It infuriated me. No means no.

V: It infuriates you when people do not get the titles.

I just don't understand it.

For Mum 'no means no', except when no means yes. She once sai not to come to her exhibition opening, 'Too much trouble to get ther Later I discovered she was disappointed I wasn't there.

Once, she was giving a talk when a man came in late and sat dow 'Come in darling man,' she said, welcoming him in with a gesture c her arm.

'Who is darling man?' I asked her later.

'Who?'

'The man who came in late.'

'Oh him. Isn't he revolting. He insists on carrying my bags to ıe car.'

*

he says to V:

As I told you, I was brought up in a family where manners were nportant. A child would stand up when a grown-up came into the ɔom. We were gracious, polite and deferential to adults. You wouldn't ay that you didn't like the meal. You would say it was delicious. In onversation the woman asked the man about himself. You wouldn't xpect him to ask about you. You kept your real thoughts to yourself. he titles of my paintings are not like manners. They are my real houghts.

V: A diary of the real thoughts of an artist.

Exactly. The titles are asking, 'How do we get permission for our nnermost selves?' In fact, that is the title of a painting.

Mum was brought up in a family where one kept one's true thoughts ɔ oneself. She was brought up in a family of secrecy—the secrecy of he grandmother she never knew, the secrecy of her father's addiction ɔ morphine, the secrecy of her father's trauma from the war. I do not now how the impulse to secrecy is transmitted from one generation ɔ the next, but I do know that I inherited my mother's propensity for ecrecy without being aware that I had. It amazed me that someone ould come into a room and report on an incident on the way there, hat they could name the feeling of shock, right at that moment, rawing attention to themselves. One kept one's feelings to oneself, leferring to others.

The conditions of an artist's work enter the work. An artist in small studio will be restricted to painting small works. An artist wi only charcoal to work with will be limited by the materials availab The psychological conditions also enter the work. Those who a accustomed to secrecy may not even realise that they are withho ing some little detail, some fact that would make sense of the wo Reflecting on my own process of writing gives me some insight into explanation for my mother's process of painting.

This is my experience. You write something and then, thinki that you might have revealed too much, you hide some of it, leavi the vestige of what you wanted to say. You anticipate the guilloti striking you down: 'You can't say that. That is forbidden.' You do n even think to say what is obvious, even something the reader needs know to make sense of what you have written. You want the read to know without telling them. You assume that something deeply f is libellous or incriminating. You hide it before knowing you ha hidden it. You are withholding without knowing you are withholdi You strive to make sense with the fragments you permit yourself write. It is painstaking, time-consuming. You think you are crafti a piece of writing when in fact you are ingeniously concealing som thing that cannot be said. You feel a constant frustration between t desire to say something and the impulse to conceal.

I noticed that other writers were not so constrained. I was envio of their eloquence, wondering how they did it. I thought it was tale or something to do with writing. I did not realise I was inhibited by th self-imposed rule until I became receptive to the inner voice aski why I was making it so difficult. But then, having recognised wh I was doing, I did not release myself from the straitjacket, flinging it o in the liberation of release. It was an effort to remove it. It had becom attached. I looked for guides from other writers to give me permissio to write—women writers who had returned from the silence of th ep. The freedom of release was shadowed by mourning, mourning e years of having inhibited myself.

It was suggested that this was a form of sabotage. As I understand 'sabotage' would involve taking the scissors to the work, savagely tting it into pieces, leaving a trail of blood in its wake. This sabo- ge is creative. It involves a huge amount of laborious work, saying mething and then retracting most of it, concealing what might be o private.

I recognise the sabotage in my mother's work. An ornate letter 'A' ats across the painting called *Know Thyself*. 'What is the letter A?' sk my mother.

'Can't you see? It's the self.'

I wonder if A is for artist, the self that writes the letter A. It is not vious to me. It is to my mother. I assume that, like me, she is leaving o much space between the dots for the reader to join up. She knows w the motifs floating across the canvas connect to the titles but is ystified that others cannot make out the connection.

She says to V:

My paintings are not for the ordinary viewer but I could never nderstand why they were not understood by the art world. I didn't nderstand what I was doing wrong.

I had applied for a grant for a painting to be made into a tapestry. y work was ideally suited to this medium with its straight lines and early delineated patches of colour. A tapestry had already been ade of my work. I wrote the application, draft after draft explain- g my ideas about transposing a painting into a tapestry. Various the children offered to type up the application but I said that my ndwriting was perfectly acceptable and when they pointed out mething called 'the selection criteria' I told them I wasn't going to nswer that incomprehensible rubbish. I didn't understand it. I wasn't en on the shortlist.

V: Perhaps you were sabotaging your work or perhaps you fe entitled to receive the grant despite not following the applicatio guidelines.

I don't know. That ridiculous form to fill in, that stupid woma whose work had been chosen. And then there was that woman wh had befriended me, asking me for help. She was very polite an gracious but she was doing these simplistic landscapes out of som sort of fabric and weaving and pearls. Very decorative but not real serious. She had approached an art gallery in Berlin to exhibit h work. I wouldn't dream of doing such a thing. My work was far mo serious than hers. I had given her advice and there she was getting a exhibition in Berlin with these decorative things she was making.

V: She dared to do what you would not permit yourself.

And Emily, my sister. Twelve years she took to finish her unive sity degree which should have taken six years. Dad paid for her stay in the university college, paying the fees every year she faile I wouldn't dream of failing. And then there was John's friend Eliz beth Summons, just a fundraiser for the gallery school, one of thos society ladies who dresses up for lunch. Not a serious person. Joh was enchanted with her, flattered that she bought a painting whe not many other people did. A week after John died she gave me a ros bush called 'first love' with a card saying, 'In memory of John'. I mea I ask you.

V: You are struggling with your envy.

No no, it wasn't envy.

In her funeral speech Mum tells us that 'she knew from experienc and humiliation that the seven deadly sins applied to her' but when names the sin of envy she denies it. In wondering about her capaci for insight into herself, I recalled the burning of Dad's portrait of Ann Purves. 'I don't know why Anne had to say that she burnt the portra She should have said she'd loaned it and then it disappeared. If sh ıd said that, John would have kept exhibiting at the gallery, bringing commissions from the sales.'

It surprised me that Mum did not see the burning as punishment to ɔd for a portrait the sitter didn't like. She was not a stranger to the easures of punishment as revenge. On letting her know that we were ɔt extensions of a doll, the four of us daughters had received pages ıd pages of letters, the pen running away with her, one vitriolic insult 'ter another. Her punishment was not often spoken directly where it ould elicit a response. It was written in the title of a painting, a letter, report to someone else. I hear her saying, 'This idiot man V thinks he ıows all about me but he doesn't. All this rubbish he goes on with.'

*

ɔr the next week V has let her know that he won't be there. She forɜts and waits for thirty minutes. In the next session she says:

You weren't here last week.

V: I am sorry, I did remind you.

Well, you weren't here.

V: You are angry with me.

No, I'm not angry. Sometimes I just wonder whether anybody cares. barely sold enough paintings to cover the cost of the exhibition. I onder if anything I do is worthwhile. All my paintings may as well ɔ into the rubbish bin for all that anybody cares.

My mother despairs that for all the attention her work has received, 'may as well go into the rubbish bin', and yet she ensures that it ill be lasting, using proper paints, proper canvases, varnishing and 'ames. I tell her that Van Gogh did not get worthy recognition until fter his death and neither did any number of women artists whose ork remains undiscovered. It does not reassure her.

She tells V:

I really should have done better, considering my advantages. mean, Dad was a very substantial person. A very serious person, ver respected in the medical world. He had a name, a reputation. All I'v done is paint pictures which only a few people buy.

V: You are comparing yourself unfairly with your father. He wa not raising four children. He was not doing the work of supporting husband. He was a doctor, you were an artist; very different offers t the world.

As I said, Dad was a very substantial person.

V: What would it take to see yourself as a substantial person, to se your considerable achievements, to see yourself as worthwhile?

It's all just poppycock to me. I don't understand this airy-fair nonsense. It's just a waste of time. I could be painting. I don't eve know why I'm here.

She doesn't turn up to the next two sessions and doesn't ring to sa she isn't coming.

In the next session she says to V:

I thought you might not be here.

V: You were punishing me. You were punishing me for inviting yo to see your own goodness, your own achievements.

She says nothing.

V: You could hear the respected critic who said, 'That is the mos erotic drawing I have ever seen.' You could hear advice from the ma who suggested longer titles; and yet, you find it difficult to hear advic suggesting that you have greater respect for your own work, that yo see your work as significant, that you see yourself as significant.

I don't know.

After a long silence she says: You are not my father.

V: Perhaps you are punishing me for not being your father.

As she gets up to leave, he notices that she is quietly weeping. He uts his arm gently around her shoulder and says, 'I will see you at our ext session.'

*

um's paintings were inextricably a part of the house. She got up on e ladder and painted the walls the same grey, purple, olive-green, ue as her paintings. Objects in the house appeared in the paintings: a oorknob, the back of a chair, a shoe. I recognised the 'withdrawal' of e titles as Dad's withdrawal with depression. When Dad had demen-a, a painting was named *The Inhabitant Has Gone*.

One Sunday afternoon not long after Dad died, I visited Mum with e grandchildren. We brought her a CD player. With no horizontal urface free of household objects, I set up the ironing board and it was om there that we heard the voice of Joan Sutherland singing *Lucia i Lammermoor*. As the late afternoon approached darkness, Mum gave o sign of wanting us to leave and as the time stretched on, I felt the nticipation that something ominous would happen. Then I remembered at Dad had died. He would not be coming in from the studio asking me hy I was still there and why Mum was not getting the dinner.

After Dad's death Mum was free of his demands. She had the house herself without Dad's grumblings about the décor she selected. ometimes journalists came to the house to interview Mum about ad's work or her own. After the first of these interviews, I asked Mum ow it went. 'I'm not into that Heide rubbish,' she said, referring to the tories of the private lives of the artists and benefactors who gathered t a place known as Heide. '"Private is private, public is public," I told he journalist.' She was warning *me* not to say anything about the rivate life of our family.

In marrying Dad, Mum had defied her family but in advocating rivate is private', she was continuing her family's rule of protecting the reputation of the important man. Until the journalist had cor to the house, there was no need to articulate the rule. It occurred me that we think we are escaping what we wish to escape from o childhood but we carry with us what has imprisoned us.

When journalists visiting the house wrote up an interview, th might respectfully refer to the 'cosily cluttered home'. I had liv in that 'cosily cluttered' home, or rather an earlier incarnation of I knew where to find the cups and saucers. I knew the location of t secret drawer where Mum's jewellery was hidden.

My description starts with the front door which opens into open-plan sitting room. Mum's chair faces the television. Almc every horizontal surface is covered with an accumulation of boo newspapers, knitting, coats, concert programs, vases of dried lavend the current TV guide. A Chinese bowl from an ancient dynasty sits the sideboard alongside a pair of nail scissors and bandaids spilli out from the box. Walking down a short passageway, we enter t kitchen–living room.

The kitchen benches are covered with a collection of jars, bott bowls, packets of tea, raisin bread, a basket bursting with plastic ba The only blank space is a chopping board on which is placed a sha knife and the powdery remnants of a pill chopped into quarters. long dining-room table holds a collection of vases containing wilti or dried flowers, often including a once-magnificent bouquet, a g for opening an exhibition. Cobwebs hold the petals of dried-up ros together; petals fall onto the table. A recently picked rose or daph might be placed in a glass vase near the end of the table, visible fro my mother's armchair, a designer chair covered in a cabbage-gre suede-velvety fabric.

The little coffee table cluttered with books and papers sits betwe the two designer chairs, one for Mum and the other for the visitor sit having lunch.

Through an open door one glimpses into what is known as 'the inting room'. This is where Mum works on her painting. The floor is rely visible. It is covered with layers of drawing and tracing paper ırked with geometric pencil lines. A narrow pathway leads from the orway to the swivel chair within reach of a small table holding tubes paints, paintbrushes, paint rags. The eye is drawn to the canvas cured to the easel. Geometrical markings cover the canvas, some loured in a musty olive-green, greyish-blue, mauve-purple. The inting shows a superb refinement of skill, painted with control, with reful deliberation. If it is nearing completion, four or five phrases ɔuld be handwritten on a piece of paper sticky-taped to the easel.

Nearly; but Not. You're not what I thought you were. He Thinks He Knows. She thinks she Doesn't. If He doesn't get it, there's Nothing to Get.

A visitor might see the house as that of an eccentric artist who had ɔre important things to do than tidy up. She might be wondering, ɔw can you live in this clutter? What's with all the dead flowers?' ıe might notice the packet of no-brand-name biscuits haphazardly aced alongside the designer glass vase. She might notice the frayed ges of the handkerchief clutched in the artist's hand, identifying a ece of torn-off Actil sheet. She would not know that somewhere in e house one could find fine embroidered handkerchiefs, linen tea wels, bath towels of Egyptian cotton, gifts from children and grandildren never used.

The house is like a labyrinth, an art installation. The artist in her inting room is in the centre of the labyrinth, spinning her web ound her.

The British artist Tracey Emin created an installation *My Bed*. Her ımade bed was removed, transported, rearranged and placed into an t gallery. Crowds lined up to stare at the tumbled sheets, used tissues, rty underwear, cigarettes, empty vodka bottles, condoms, perhaps held the fantasy of the drama that had created the tableaux before them.

After his death, Francis Bacon's shambled mess of a studio was d mantled, transported and reinstalled in the country of his birth. The private spaces made public may have promised to reveal the mind the artist, as if somewhere amidst that disorder the mystery to the a could be found.

Very often, as I drove towards my mother's house, the thoug would strike me: 'Who am I to visit Helen Brack, Helen Maudsley?' I a not a journalist, a gallery director, a curator. If I were not her daught I would not be paying her a visit. I am not a person of significance.

During the visit, Mum's conversation would be punctuated uncensored asides. 'She asked the most daft questions.' 'So and so just an idiot.' 'He's just a nobody.' 'She thinks she knows about John work, but she doesn't.' 'He fancies himself as a real artist.' 'It's ju decorative what she's doing. It's not serious work.' 'She's just pand ing to what other people want.'

Sometimes I would offer my opinion. 'Well, her work is in a diff ent genre from yours, Mum. It's a more accessible genre; besides, sh is a performance artist. Your work demands a different way of lookin

Driving home I would find myself consumed by a dull nothingne I would see myself as worthless. It was not until a real conversatio with another human being that my sense of myself would be restore I could not explain it. It's not as if my mother had pointed her fing at me *telling* me I was worthless, and I knew it wasn't just that I wa looking at myself through her eyes. It took me a long time to realis that the worthlessness I felt in the presence of my mother was wh she felt about herself. In seeking a connection with her, I made myse susceptible to the worthlessness she unconsciously transmitted, ar which temporarily relieved her of it.

She tells V:

I loved the house and garden, painting the rooms, selecting th furniture and the objects in the house. Early in John's career, whe e children were little, I would spend days tidying up for an important visitor who had come to see John about his work. After all that dying up, I remember one of the visitors saying, 'How nice to see a ouse so lived in.'

I was interested in cooking and loved making meals for people. ated it when a meal was lovingly made and considered, but accepted the recipient as trash. I never got over the time it took two days to epare and cook a dinner with a duck. The two guests picked and oked at the dishes and after the dinner the lady of the couple said, really don't like that sort of cooking. I prefer plain duck with apple uce and mashed potatoes and peas. I'm only being honest.' John ought it was funny. I felt angry and defeated and never forgot it. e next day I got up, rallied myself and did everything again—the ildren, the painting and what needed to be done for the household. could never be said that I was a warrior, which John certainly was.

V: Perhaps John could not have been a warrior without your help eparing him for battle, your consolation if the battle was lost, and our encouragement for the battle that would follow.

That was my job. I did it meticulously. I did all the business side of it, arning John not to give away a drawing, telling those gallery people at we would not be their stupid unpaid servants, you know. Even ough we were both doing the same work painting pictures, my work as not given anything like the attention that John's work was given. I ondered if it was because I was a woman artist. In those days, gallery irectors supported men artists who also had wives or girlfriends to lly them along. When women's liberation came to Melbourne in the te 1960s, women artists formed a group. I went along, hopeful, but turned out that these women artists were against the men artists st for being men. They didn't want to be taken seriously. They just anted to be given the status of great artist, of high achiever—what any of the men artists wanted also, and which I had contempt for.

V: So you didn't join up with the women artists.

No, I didn't join up. I wasn't at all interested in shooting down th men artists I admired.

V: One of whom was your husband.

As both Helen Brack, wife of the artist, and Helen Maudsley, artis more often than not Mum was invited to artist events as the wife o the artist, thereby receiving an entrée into a world from which othe 'women artists' were excluded. If Dad did not want to go to one o these events, Mum went alone but the delight when someone showe an interest in her work could turn to indignation if it turned out tha they were simply 'cosying' up to her, as she said, to find out somethin about Dad.

Several years after his death, she was speaking about her painting when another panellist turned to her and asked, 'Is it true that you ar John Brack's wife?'

'Never heard of him,' she said.

She says to V:

As I said, I didn't want to shoot down men artists whom I admire And I certainly wasn't going to kowtow to John. I remember the firs time he said he didn't want to go to an artist party. He was very take aback when I said I would go without him. He expected me to stay a home keeping him company watching the television. I loved gettin dressed up and going out. I loved talking to the other artist wives. I als had the credibility as an artist myself. Sometimes someone would as me why John wasn't there as if I wasn't entitled to be there myself.

V: You felt that you belonged.

If John had come, he would have sulked all the way home.

In public Mum would claim her rightful place as an artist and a artist wife. In private Dad's needs took priority. When he was tol to stop drinking, Mum worried that if we were drinking wine o hristmas day, he would help himself to the bottle. It had been a lot of ffort to get him off the grog, so I understood why Mum didn't want im tempted.

A few days before Christmas, Mum told me how she had bought everal bottles of mineral water and different-coloured fruit juice, nixing them together in her kitchen laboratory. 'If I pour this into a vine glass, John will think it is wine. He won't know the difference.'

I assumed that Dad would be drinking Mum's concoction while we vere drinking the real stuff, but it turned out that this was not to be he case. On Christmas day, we were offered what looked like white vine, red wine and rosé presented in wine glasses on a tray. If Dad vas not permitted alcohol none of us would be permitted, including Mum herself.

She says to V:

Last night I woke up in the middle of the night, feeling guilty about ny murderous thoughts about John. I remembered my fury with him or getting dementia, for not looking after himself, for needing all my ttention. And then I lay awake feeling guilty about any number of hings to do with the children.

V: You are tormenting yourself.

At least when I am painting, I am not feeling guilty.

Mum yearns to be free of the 'everyday guilt'. I doubt that she felt uilt about not protecting us from Dad's undermining. She endured it erself. No one protected her.

I remember one dinnertime. Dad, sitting up his end of the kitchen able, eating his steak, Mum sitting up her end, the four of us in the niddle, finishing our chops. Dad was drunk. 'Look at your mother. Look at her. Isn't she despicable. Isn't she disgusting.' None of us could peak but Mum found her voice. 'Stop it John. Stop it. Not in front of he children.'

Dad would scoff at the everyday encounters that gave Mum ple ure. He did not have the temperament or the inclination to savo what delighted Mum and to share it with her. To her disappointme he refused to accompany her on several trips overseas visiting the a galleries. She wrote wonderful letters, seven or eight pages of wor crammed onto the page. *The café is run by a darling little German m with real old-world courtesy...The guards have the most glamoro dashing uniforms, pale-grey with an extraordinary comic version o Russian fur hat.*

After Dad's death, I had imagined that for the first time in her l Mum could spend uninterrupted time on her own work and things s liked doing. I had not anticipated that a mythical aura is bequeath to the recently deceased artist, an aura that entices the wife of t artist to make a space for herself in the halo of this mystique. Mu conscientiously responded to the invitations to promote Dad's wo giving talks, writing essays and opening exhibitions. She could reli the status of the venerated wife of the artist unencumbered by t presence of the artist himself.

She was free of her duties as a wife, but she was also free to be authority on Dad's work. She spent hours not so much *looking* at h paintings but *deciphering* them, seeking to elicit his intentions as if t paintings were, like hers, seeking to be 'deciphered'. I do not know ho she convinced herself that *The Block*, a painting of a butcher's blo was a reference to the Holocaust. When asked for justification fro someone in the audience, 'Did you talk to John about his paintin she retaliated with, 'Of course we did.' Later she would refer to t 'idiot' who asked the question. It was not just the appropriation of t Holocaust that alarmed us children, but the fact that she had attribut it to Dad. If we dared to query what we suggested were *her* interpre tions of Dad's paintings, she would retaliate with something like, 'Nc I know why people ask me why John hated his children so much.'

She says to V:

After John's death I was asked to give talks about his work and 'ite articles for auction catalogues. I took this job very seriously, ıdying the paintings, taking notes, spending hours writing up what e painting was about. After giving a talk it was often disappointing. ople would ask the most daft questions. They wanted to know ıether John discussed his work with me, whether I had read what he .d written, whether we had the same studio and watched each other ınting. It was insulting. They didn't have a clue.

V: Perhaps they were wondering how you knew John's meaning of e painting.

They weren't. They were just being stickybeaks.

V: As you said, you knew what the painting was about from looking it, not from what John said about it.

I knew what John meant. I mean, the nicest thing he ever did was that last painting of the five Pinocchio figures. It was a way of anking all of us for all the work we put into his career.

V: Just the fact of there being five figures?

It was obvious that the five figures represented the mother and the ur children and that in putting us into the painting he was thanking for what we had done for his work.

V: You needed John to make this acknowledgement. You wanted be seen. You wanted to be acknowledged. And John made that knowledgement.

No no, you idiot. I know what John meant.

One Sunday afternoon Mum gave a talk on Dad's painting *The Bar* the National Gallery of Victoria. The painting depicts a woman at e bar with a mirror behind her. The mirror reflects the men drinking. vase of poppies is on the bar. Well before the beginning of the talk e four of us daughters had seated ourselves in the audience along with several husbands and grandchildren. We were there to give h our moral support and to boost the numbers in the audience as Mu worried there would not be sufficient people turning up. She co menced reading the talk. Later she sent me a copy.

'Let's look at *The Bar* 1954. John was thirty-four and I w twenty-seven when he painted *The Bar*. In 1954 our fourth daught was born, our first having been born in 1949, so John's suburban hon life was dominated by babies and small children. Look at *The Bar* aga Can you see how all the hats at the top look like suburban roof top Stare again and can you see how those two light bits form a face?'

The face eluded me. I nervously wondered what others in the au ence were thinking.

'Look at the barmaid; can you see how the man on the left match her? A husband and wife. Can you see how the shape of the vase womb-shaped? The bottles relate via the V shape to the barmaid; a they children?'

I wondered if Mum felt unnerved by the silence of the audien She would have no way of reading whether they were following her

'Then there are the flowers whose stems you hardly see but who petals tremble, as it were. Is this not unlike the tremble of the embry inside the womb? See the exaggerated size of the slurping man in th centre, and is this not like the baby learning to drink from a cup aft weaning? The barmaid is the mother, the mopper-up of mess. See ho the glasses become the children, cleaning, and is that forceful V imag of the beer tap on the right side of the picture to do with engenderir and potency?'

I dared not think what Dad would make of this.

'This picture is about the continuation of human life, but was nev seen as such.'

She stopped reading and appealed for a response. 'This is intere ing, is it not?'

I nodded. Others were nodding. She continued until the talk con-
uded, the audience clapped enthusiastically and then questions
llowed.

What *is* interesting is what is not said. The woman in *The Bar* splays her hands. Hands are very difficult to draw. Mum does not ıy that she made time from looking after the baby and three small ıildren to pose as a model for the hands. She concluded her talk with, his picture is about the continuation of human life, but was never een as such.'

To my knowledge, she had not seen it as such herself until Dad's omment many years after he painted *The Bar* when she returned om seeing a newborn grandchild.

'When I told John that I didn't understand why I was weeping over e new baby, he said, "You know what that is? That is the continu- ion of human life."' I wondered if she had remembered something ad said about the Holocaust and attributed that to the painting called ıe *Block*.

After the talk, knowing Mum's need for reassurance, I told her ow interesting it was and how well it was received, feeling the dis- ıste of colluding in something I considered ludicrously improbable. ad said himself that *The Bar* was a comment on Manet's painting *Bar at the Folies-Bergère*. His focus was not on the mother of his ıildren inside the house; it was on creating a place for himself in the istory of Art.

She says to V:

John's painting *The Bar* is obviously not just a painting of a armaid. It's a picture of me as the mother, the mopper-up of mess. 's John's acknowledgement of all the work that I was doing as a ıother.

V: You looked at the painting, and you saw yourself reflected back. ou needed John to see you and you saw that in the painting.

No no, that was what John had intended.

V: In not wishing to confront your disappointment that John di not thank you for what you did for his work, you told yourself story that he had acknowledged you in the painting. In telling it to a audience and hearing their applause, you could convince yourself tha John had given you the thanks that you craved.

No no, it wasn't like that.

V: If you release yourself from this self-deception, you will face th disappointment that John never told you what you meant to him.

No no. That is just rubbish.

And then, after a long pause, she says:

At least you're not saying what John would say.

V: What is that?

Can't you get that into your fat head. You nong.

*

In the time between the visits with V, I want to believe that she wi consider what V is saying. I want to believe that she will weep for th loss that arose when Dad had dementia, for the loss after his death an for her disappointment that he never thanked her for all that she di for him.

In the next session she says:

I like to think that if John didn't get dementia he would hav thanked me for all that I had done for him. He never thanked Dad fc getting him the job at Melbourne Grammar.

V: You did an extraordinary amount of work for John's career.

Well, that's just what was expected of a wife. The wife looked afte the husband as the breadwinner.

V: You are disappointed that John did not acknowledge all the wor you put into his career but when I acknowledge you, you dismiss m s if you are resisting the very thing you seek. You belittle me for raising you, offering you comfort as if you are not worthy of it. You nut me off. You find it difficult to name your feelings. You either say don't know' or deny them. You are your own worst enemy with your ppetite for self-abnegation.

Well, who are you? I've never heard anyone speak to me like that.

In the next session she says:

I don't know. I wish I didn't feel this guilt, not just everyday guilt, uilt that I have done something wrong.

V: Perhaps you are feeling guilt that you have not lived up to the npossible demands you put on yourself. Perhaps you are feeling ne unknown guilt that your parents passed on. The sins of the father assed onto the child.

Whatever it is, I just want relief from the feeling of the guilt.

V: What would it take to absolve yourself of the guilt?

I don't know. Now I feel guilty that I am taking up your time.

*

t's an honour to have an exhibition at the NGV,' I said to Mum after he opening of her exhibition.

'Oh yes, it is an honour but it's tedious what you have to do beforeand. I just hope I've got everything right.'

Respectful articles were written about her work in major newsapers. She was interviewed on the radio, invited to give talks about er work. Despite the attention, she could not be coaxed into enjoying he success.

'There's been a lot of interest in your exhibition, Mum. It's fantastic, ll the publicity.'

'I'll just be glad when the wretched thing is over.'

'It's marvellous, Mum,' I said, striving to generate some enthusias 'So many people have been to the exhibition and Sasha wrote th lovely review. "A profound exhibition", he called it.'

'Oh yes, that *was* a nice review but what about the friends?'

'What about the friends?'

'Well, [name of friend] said, "The paintings are beautiful Helen, b I don't know what they mean." It's disgusting. And then a womar went to school with invited me to lunch. She said she didn't und stand the titles. She asked me to explain them. I mean, I ask you, t idiot. Some people are just daft. To think she had been some sort professor at the university.'

'But lots of people have been terribly impressed. And you did that amazing work without the support of Dad.'

In the silence after, I could see her considering her response.

'But you wouldn't say that to anybody, would you?'

To say that would damage the reputation of the important man.

How does she describe this to V?

Well, finally I did have an exhibition at the NGV with three oth women artists. You just have to go along with what the curator wan All this nonsense they go on with. It's so far removed from the actu job of painting. John hated that sort of thing, but you have to do I didn't see what all the fuss was about. It takes so much time aw from painting. I was just glad when the wretched thing was ov People say the most daft things. Do you get your ideas from dream I mean, I ask you. One of the other women artists was traipsi around the exhibition with her mother and father, talking about t paintings. I wish my father had seen my paintings and understo them.

V: What would it mean if your father had seen your paintings ar understood them?

It would mean that I wouldn't have self-doubt.

V: You invested him with that authority.

Whatever that means. I don't know.

Silence.

When John had self-doubt, it was my job to tell him not to be so ɬiculous.

V: It wouldn't occur to you that John could relieve you of lf-doubt.

I don't know. I never wavered in my belief in John as an artist. In s preoccupation with his work, he didn't have much time for mine. ɜ was not an easy person to live with. No one really knew the diffiɪlties of living with his depression and his drinking.

V: You could have left him.

Oh no. I couldn't do that. Not after that enormous effort in the early ɪys getting John to be successful. I would not leave him for some ɪung popsy to come in, swooping him up, getting all the rewards.

V: What were the rewards?

Oh, I don't know. His success. The fact that he was seen as a sigficant artist. The respect he was given, that little bit more money at came into the household. I am extremely glad that John has been ccessful. He was the right person with the right contribution at the ght time.

V: And you were the right person to support him. His success was ɪur reward for the work you put into his career.

It was very important for John to be successful. In those days ost wives supported their husbands. It's just what you did. That's hat my mother did. You just made do with the space you were given. hn had a painting room in the house. My workspace was a board ɪer a desktop in the sitting room. When John became head of the ɪllery school, he no longer needed work space at home, so for the first ne in my life I had a painting room of my own. I didn't have to clear everything up at the end of the day. I could do bigger works. I cou paint in oil paints not just watercolours.

V: Your painting had been limited by the space you had available

That's just how it was. I knew from very early on that I wou take a different approach to painting from John. While maintaini integrity of the task, John set his sights on meshing with the publ whereas people like me were deemed amateurs because we didn't ai to fit in with viewers. John needed to fit in with viewers. He need to mesh with the public in order to sell paintings so we would ha enough money to live on. I was just doing what I was meant to do supporting his career.

V: As you said, you had not aimed to fit in with viewers. In ensuri that your work would require more from the viewer, you guarante that it would receive less attention than John's. If more attention ha been given to your work, John would have seen you as taking th place that both you and he had designated to him.

No no no, it wasn't like that. John was a very significant arti You're just like the others, too stupid to see what I am getting at, readi into it what you want to see. I supported John not because of any goc ness but because it was in my interest to do so. It was terribly *much* my interest that John was a success. He would have hated not bei successful. I would have had to cope with his sulking and his misery, h complaints, his moaning about wanting to give up. He would have mac our home life unbearable, not just for me but for the children.

V: You created elusive and enigmatic works that ask a lot fro others to understand. Perhaps unconsciously, you ensured that yo work was not readily understood because if more interest was give to it, John would see you as taking his rightful place, and in his woun edness he would have made your home life unbearable.

No no no. I wanted to paint what you call 'elusive ar enigmatic' works.

V: Perhaps you could not have created these enigmatic works if you d not have the security of John's shadow in which to hide. While 'otesting against being in John's shadow, perhaps you are overlook-g the necessity to hide in his shadow.

That's just rubbish.

*

: a concert Mum will loudly proclaim: 'The men cellists are just better .an the women.' One of her granddaughters is a cellist.

In the second week of interviews for my daughter's first published ɔok, Mum rang me to tell me that, 'Alice should stop all that nonsense ıblicity. She will be getting too big for her boots.'

If this was her response to her granddaughters, what would it have ɜen for her daughters? We must have known not to venture into that ɔace. She may not have said it explicitly but this is the message I ·ceived: 'If others want to be recognised, let them have it; they want more than you do.' And yet, she herself had never forgotten that uth Muir got 93.75 for the music exam and she got 93.45.

*

ıe says to V:

People don't get the titles of my paintings and you don't seem to get 'hat I am saying when I tell you that it was very important to John to ɜ successful.

V: Perhaps you see the public space as belonging to the man. You :apple with your envy of women who dare to take up the space that ɔu do not allow yourself to take. The woman who had an exhibition ı Berlin for those decorative pieces she was making, not a serious rtist like yourself. The women artists who wanted to be 'great artists', 'ho had ambition which you had contempt for.

Well, so many women artists just do works that are decorativ and pretty. Art isn't about beauty. It's about being serious. I just don understand why serious people don't see the seriousness of my work

V: Perhaps 'serious' for you requires untangling a complicated maz In paring back the image and in writing longer titles, you were erec ing a very sophisticated scaffolding around yourself. After spendin so much effort devising such a scaffolding, it would be too confrontin to face the fact that you could take it down. When you see others nc putting themselves through such an elaborate process, it insults yo How can they get away with it? It affronts you that others are not co ering themselves up as you are. Furthermore, they are getting awa with it. You are protecting yourself against being known.

Long silence.

I recently did a series of four paintings called *There, but Protectin Against. Retiring into one's Head. And Ambiguity.*

V: Underneath the 'retiring into the head and ambiguity' there is small child crying out to be seen and known and loved and understoo

A young man was asked to clean a chandelier. It took him hour to remove each piece of dangling glass, clean it and return it to it designated place. On being told to remove each piece of glass and pu it back the right way around, he said, 'I'm out of here. I don't want n prism sentence.'

In erecting the elaborate scaffolding around herself, I see m mother as giving herself a prism sentence, resisting knowledge of th forces that had led her into the prism.

*

After Dad's death Mum received the gift of a novel which starts wit a widow calling on her widowed neighbour, wondering if he, too, i lonely and if so, would he consent to sleeping with her—not for sex bu for keeping their souls company at night. Mum could not be drawn o iscussing the novel, but the title *Our Souls At Night* must have struck chord for, since receiving the novel, 'Our Souls' appeared in the titles f her paintings.

Our Souls that meet; our Souls together.

Our Souls; not our Selves. And the Shoe. 2019

Our Souls, Together and in Communication.

Here and Now. For a Moment. 2019

At a birthday dinner in her eighties, Mum tells us that she has an nnouncement to make. 'I have a new friend.' She leads us to expect ıat the new friend is like the widowed neighbour seeking a way out f loneliness at night. 'Every day on my walk my new friend is waiting ɔr me at the top of the hill. Sometimes he is not there.'

Her new friend is the moon. He appears in some of her paintings.

Looking down, Looking up at, Looking into. The Quarter Moon, The Half Moon, and The Full Moon. The Leaf is the Lips. 2022

Mum finds what she is looking for. I want her to find what she is ot looking for.

She did several paintings named *Shostakovich Waltz No. 2.* I want to take her out of 'retiring into one's head and ambiguity'. I want him ɔ gently take her by the hand, pull her up from the chair, place one and on her shoulder, the other around her waist and twirl her around ɔ the music of Shostakovich's Waltz No. 2. I want her to collapse in he chair, exuberant, exhilarated. Given that V would not swirl her round in a waltz, knowing she would lose her balance, I will have to nd something else to release her.

She tells V:

On my trip overseas, I went to the art museum in Philadelphia very day for a week, getting to know the museum guards, chatting to hem every day. On the last day of my visit, they invited me into the ffice where I was surprised to see that they had given me a farewell arty with cups of tea and cakes. I didn't understand it. I thought they nust have mistaken me for someone of significance.

V: Why else would they be giving you a party? They are telling yo you are a person of significance. They are showing appreciation f your friendly chats.

After a minor brush with another car, Mum told us the passwo for her bankcard 'in case anything happens to me'. I recognised t initials of the four of us daughters and the order of our birth. 'What the Q in the middle?' I ask. 'Can't you see? The Q is for queen.' Despi her sense of herself as insignificant, I wondered if she also saw hers as Q for queen.

Mum's doctor had advised her to have a daily walk after a h replacement. Since then, she had refused the advice to have a wa ing aid, subsequently falling several times at home and in the stre We had given her a walking stick, a walking stick with a fold-up se attached, a walking frame. We considered sending her a postcard Dad's painting, *A Walking Stick Makes a Good Companion*. 'The Que has a walking frame,' I said, 'so did Dame Elisabeth Murdoch,' a wom Mum admired and was flattered to be mistaken for. Her response to question from an aged-care assessor: 'No, I don't get mood swings' a then, her voice rising to a crescendo, 'I get thoroughly pissed off wh one of the children suggests that I need a walking stick or a walki frame.' On our insistence she conceded to having an alarm butt around her neck.

Mum interpreted *The Bar* as a commentary on her. She saw hers as the woman at the bar, 'the mopper-up of mess'. Dad's painti *The Chase* is of three girls running. We recognised ourselves. I ha no illusion that Dad actually *saw* us and yet when Mum offered t painting to the NGV as a gift, we felt that she was giving away a pie of us, a painting that said we meant something to Dad. On hearing o objections, Mum reluctantly withdrew the offer.

Several years later, we heard that she had offered it to the Art Gal-'y of Ballarat. Again, we asked her to reconsider.

She tells V:

On Friday morning, all four of the children came to see me, not for :riendly visit but to persuade me not to give away John's painting *.e Chase*. I don't know why they thought there was any point in ming to see me. I had already made up my mind. The darling man the gallery had already accepted the painting, I could hardly go .ck and say he couldn't have it. On and on they went about how the .inting meant something to them just because three of them were it. They had never been so united. If I had kept the painting, they ɔuld have squabbled over whose turn to have it and for how long. I said, the Ballarat gallery is the best place for it. It is a significant .inting of John's. It deserves to be seen by more people than in a mily home. Anyway, I was jolly glad when they left. As I told them, s my painting, I can do what I like with it.'

V: You found the power to defeat them.

Six months after the gift of *The Chase*, the four of us received a oup email from Mum's contact at the Ballarat gallery. He was writ-g to tell us that the Ballarat gallery was honoured to welcome our ther's wonderful painting into the gallery collection. He was 'reach-g out' to see whether any or all of us would be interested in speaking ith *The Age* which would run the story 'as an exclusive'. He proposed at a photograph of the gallery director standing next to *The Chase* ɔuld be 'more interesting' with us included. We were warmly invited lunch and a tour of the gallery.

The next day Mum asked me about the email from her Ballarat pal, 'ofessing not to know what it was about despite having given him ır email addresses. I told her that we had clarified that the gift was

from her and not from the Brack family, and that we had declined t
invitation to take part in the publicity for *The Chase*.

Later that day I received an automatic text message from Mum alarm button. A flurry of texts let me know that Mum had fallen the street, that she had a head laceration, and that a bystander h rung an ambulance. A photo of the scene showed a forlorn, shrivell figure slumped in the middle of the road, head bowed, blood trickli down her face. Blankets cover her legs, a bandage towel is wrapp around her head. A woman wearing protective gloves is dabbing her face. Four or five people are standing around the seated figure. was almost 5 pm on a Friday afternoon.

The ambulance arrived and Mum was taken to the hospital. Ch lotte waited with her for several hours in emergency.

The next day I received a photo of the front page of *The Couri* The entire front page was given over to a photograph of the Ballar gallery director standing next to Dad's painting, the headline declarin 'Ballarat Wins The Chase'. A short paragraph (story page six) stat 'The artist is renowned for his dour portraits of ordinary people th normally sell for millions but this key work has been donated by t artist's wife, Helen.' As readers were turning the pages of the newsp per, the artist's wife Helen was slumped in the middle of a suburb street, blood trickling from her head, having ignored the advice of h four daughters to have a walking stick, the same four daughters who pleading she triumphantly ignored in donating *The Chase*.

I recalled the studio portrait of the two-year-old, dressed in a sat frock with Peter Pan collar, hair brushed, a bow tied in her hair, arm clasping a teddy bear. I recalled a photograph of the young woma taken by celebrated photographer Athol Shmith: hair permed, pear around her neck, formally posed in a photograph required of a daug ter of the Melbourne Establishment. I look again at the photo of t woman fallen in the street. A crumpled figure slumped, a banda wrapped around her head instead of the crown befitting a woma ho saw herself as Q for queen. There was something tragically King ear-ish about it. Dad would see the little comedy. I can't see what at is.

She comes in to see V, a blue-black bruise down her face.

V: Oh, what happened?

It's nothing really. It looks much worse than it is. One minute I was alking across the road and the next minute I was sitting down with omeone wrapping something around my head. People were standing ound me. I don't know why they didn't help me up. I didn't ask them be there.

V: You didn't ask them to be there, but you created a situation here they would put themselves there, putting yourself at the mercy the public for help.

You're just as bad as John. I woke up in the middle of the night earing him saying, 'Serves you right.' I am constantly thinking, how *ould* I have done that, and why on *earth* didn't I do that? Why did I ot hear what others were saying until after a disaster? Why could see in hindsight but not in foresight?

V: So what is your explanation?

I just didn't think it would happen to me, not if I was especially areful.

V: You thought you would be immune to what other mortals suffer.

I don't know.

V: What is stopping you from asking for help? What is stopping ou from seeing yourself as worthy of the kindness of strangers utting a bandage on your head, waiting until seeing you safely into ne ambulance, the door closed and driven off to the hospital? What stopping you from seeing yourself as worthy of a little celebration om the guards at a museum, showing their appreciation at having nade a connection with them?

I don't know. My life is peppered with omissions and inapprop ate moves and also my own ignorance and unawareness—expectir people would laugh at the funny parts of the speech I made and the ridiculed for missing the point. Expecting a friend would be please with a surprise visit and then when we arrived attacked by savag dogs, terrifying the children. Realising that the present I had give was somehow not right. More and more often I regret that I haven been kinder to people, more thoughtful, more aware of other people agonies, regretting my lack of patience, thinking they should just pu themselves together as I had.

V: We can torment ourselves with regrets, indulge ourselves wit our misgivings, punish ourselves for what we did or didn't do. I ar giving you some homework, appealing to your conscientiousnes I am asking you to be kind to yourself, to see yourself as significar to recognise your achievement, to see your worthiness as a huma being.

I don't know. I am not going to be kind to myself just by sayin 'I promise to be kind to myself'.

V: Very well, let me try another approach. You asked, 'How do w get permission for our innermost selves?' I am giving you permissio to be kind to your innermost self. This is your homework, to at leas think about what I am saying.

I don't know. It all seems too much right at this moment. Ove whelming.

In the next session she says:

You will be pleased to know that I have been doing my homewor Bill Nuttall exhibited my work at Niagara Galleries. I once told him tha the only reason he shows my paintings is that this gives him access t selling John's work. 'Well, that's not actually true,' he said. 'They ar very valuable works, very significant.' Now I actually believe him.

V: That is wonderful. You are giving Bill the respect he deserves. erhaps your respect for Bill can extend to yourself, to me and to all uman beings.

After a silence she hastily brushes back a tear, gathering herself gether to say what she needs to say now.

I realise that I was very angry with Mum for depriving us of a randmother who would have loved us. I have been wondering about e guilt she must have felt, the fear of being found out, the shame of eing found out, the shame of the grandmother living in sin. I wonder hether her guilt was passed on to me. I now feel a blessing for being elieved of the guilt. I don't know how it happened.

V: Congratulations. That is marvellous.

In the next session she says:

I have been doing some research on Eddie Leonski.

V: Oh, remind me who he is.

He was found guilty of murdering several women in Melbourne in e 1940s. Dad was the psychiatrist who had been called upon to give im a psychiatric assessment. Leonski was sentenced to death. He was rrified of dying. It wasn't part of his job, but Dad made time to visit im in prison, and on the day of his execution he sat with him, holding is hand right until the end.

V: Perhaps you see me as holding your hand right until the end.

I don't want to think about the end.

V: You don't want to think about the end and yet I sense a reconciliation with yourself. As you said, you actually believed Bill when he aid your paintings were significant. You are trusting that he means hat he says. You are trusting your innermost self.

I do feel relieved to think that my paintings aren't going into the ubbish bin and all that effort has actually been worthwhile.

V: All that effort has been worthwhile.

A long silence.

V: That is wonderful. Congratulations. We have concluded o[ur] work together.

I feel a sort of sadness now, but thank you. Thank you, darling ma[n].

V: Thank you.

V helps her with her coat and then holds her to him tightly in t[he] loving warmth of an embrace.

Reflections

No one starts out in therapy knowing where it will take them. It's n
just discovering what is underlying the conflict with one's boss.

No one starts out writing knowing where it will take them. I d
not start out with this intention but now I realise that I have told n
mother's story as the story of a woman who yearns to be seen ar
loved by her father, and my father's story as the story of a man recc
ciling with his mother.

How would I tell the story of how I came to be writing theirs?

My story starts with writing letters. My mother was too busy
hear about my day so I wrote letters to her. 'Darling Darling Mumn
tomorrow we have Rilidjus Inshrukshon.' Having never heard of
man called God, I thought I was telling her about this amazing ma
she didn't know existed.

My story continues with the closest I would ever get to my fath
sitting for my portrait. As a child I sat very still thinking that if
moved, he would make a mistake. I saw him as all knowing, lookir
into me, seeing everything about me. Thirty years later I did not giv
him this omnipotence. As I sat watching him sketch, I kept my co
posure, aware of his failings, knowing he would never know very muc
about me. I wrote a letter telling him what it meant to me sitting f
the portrait.

Before he drew portraits of my children, I reassured them that they d not have to sit perfectly still. Papa would not make a mistake. I took ack-and-white photographs of the sittings, each child posed in front ' the artist sketching. After developing the negatives, I discovered at the image was not what I had seen looking through the camera. It as a scrambled incoherence of faces, hands, pens, pencils, drawings, oorways. I had neglected to take the used film out of the camera. One t of photographs was superimposed over another.

Gazing at this muddled conglomeration I heard my father's voice, ou dill.' As a way of counteracting his voice within me, I decided to int the photograph with an accompanying letter drawing attention the mistakes with comments in red in the margin.

In pre-empting my father's criticism, I was telling him that I would ot make him the judging omnipotent being. I pointed out the enig-atic mystery of the collage, a mystery that I could not have depicted ad I set out to make it.

I do not know what my father made of the photograph with its ritten commentary below, but I do know that it meant something to m. The next time I saw it, it was hung on the wall framed behind ass. A painting had been relocated to make space for it.

By putting the letter into the frame my father had given me the gift f his acknowledgement. For my sixteenth birthday he had given me .M. Forster's *Aspects of the Novel*, 'Yes, oh dear, yes, the novel tells a ory', and H.W. Fowler's *Dictionary of Modern English Usage*. Until en he had never given me a gift.

I read my father's books. He said that, originally, he wanted to be a oet but had abandoned the idea as he didn't think he had the talent. am not a poet but I have drawn on the work of poets and writers and hat they say about writing. The writer William Maxwell says, 'My other's sister told me that when my mother was twelve years old she sed to go up into the attic and "write on her novel." So perhaps I am a rojection of my mother's unlived literary life.'

Perhaps I am a projection of the unlived life of my father. Wh about the unlived life of my mother? 'But you wouldn't say that t anybody, would you?' my mother said in response to my remark th she did 'all that amazing work without the support of Dad'. For her, t 'say that' would be to cast aspersions on the reputation of the impc tant man. For me not to 'say that' would be to deny one of the force that had shaped me.

'How do we get permission for our innermost selves?' my moth asks in the title of a painting. In speaking of the private, I am givin myself permission to speak my innermost self. In speaking of the p vate, I am offering an insight into how my mother's deference to th important man had seeped into her work. In speaking of the privat I am living the unlived life of my mother.

When friends and acquaintances discover that I am the daughter two artists I am often asked, 'Do you paint?' Besides talent, there ar legacies we carry from our parents. There are 'the gaps left within u by the secrets of others, the opportunity to repair something, to mak amends, to make sense and give meaning to what is passed on to u like a baton.

'Now my journey through folklore is over...(I have) confirmation what I already suspected—folktales are real.' It is not just quotes th I am drawn to but stories that resonate.

Something had fascinated me about the story of the Japanese ma Yasuo Takamatsu who had learned scuba diving so he could go searc ing in the ocean for the body of his wife who had disappeared after th tsunami. For more than ten years he searched, putting himself in th space where his wife had disappeared.

In writing my mother and my father's dialogue with a therapis I have put myself into the vastness of the ocean between truth an fiction and where they collide. I have put myself into that spac between the death of my parents and my own death when my me ories of them will disappear. Unlike Takamatsu, I was not looking fo omething that was lost but until I came to the end of the writing, or ather the ending came to me, I did not know what would emerge from ithin the depths of the writing.

My father said that he felt atavistic guilt for being so much more nancially successful than his father. My mother was seeking atonement for her everyday guilt.

What about my own guilt? I felt guilt that my mother did not eceive the recognition for her paintings that Dad had received, having orked so hard, doing all the housework, looking after Dad and looking after us children. She tells V that she felt guilt for getting pregnant, hat it was her fault. Perhaps the guilt that I attribute to her is my guilt hat I was the child she conceived and why she subsequently had to et married.

Writing transforms the writer. In writing the scene where V mbraces my mother, I felt the warmth of his love and her need to eceive it. In receiving his love I was relieved of the sense of betraying ny mother in speaking of what she considered private. In writing and ewriting the scene where my father makes a cup of tea for his mother, felt his nervousness in pouring the water into the teapot, putting the ic Toc biscuits onto the plate, bringing in the tray. I felt his desire o offer something to his mother, to please her. As my father shed his rievances with his mother, I was shedding my grievances with him.

Now that I am nearing the end of this writing, I anticipate feeling ereft despite the achievement of having resolved something with ny mother and my father. What can I do next? I wonder what would rise if I had a conversation with the writing part of myself. But even s I prepare to ask what to do next I know that the writing has to ome from something deeper, something mysterious, something more lusive. We cannot look for it. It finds us. When asked what inspired er to write her novel, the writer said that the idea had come to her in he car on the way to her grandfather's funeral.

I know now that when we sit with the question we become rec
tive to answers that present themselves to us.

Perhaps I am looking for the girl I was. If could speak to her I wou
ask, 'Are you within me or have you gone forever?'

Postscript

In the beginning of this book I wondered what it would have been li if there was a boy in our family. I had invented a scenario where n father has a son with Sonya, a Russian dancer who has defected fro the Ballets Russes.

As the book reached its final stage I emailed Sasha Grishin who h interviewed Dad in writing *The Art of John Brack*, which had been valuable resource to me. I informed him of the forthcoming book. an email response he observes:

Writing a monograph on an artist's work is a very different ex cise to writing about a person's biography. I think that many peop have different facades when it comes to other people. I am a differe person to my wife and children than I am to my students and aga different to my artist friends. I don't think that I am consciously awa of this, but many people have told me, for example, I appear to be different person when I am speaking Russian from the person spec ing in English.

Then he says this:

Your father, for me, was an incredibly kind person. I think abo the number of times he would go down to Camberwell and buy f me a bottle of Noilly Prat extra dry vermouth when I was comir round, simply because I couldn't stand whiskey. He selected passag of poetry, esp Philip Larkin, that he wanted to discuss with me ar ould bring out paintings to talk about. This had nothing to do with ır book and continued after the book was published. He showed me a 'eat generosity of spirit and I was surprised when some other people oke of negative experiences with him. His biggest compliment was hen he said to me, if I had a son, I would have liked him to be a bit :e you.

References

Abraham, N. (1987) 'Notes on the phantom: A complement to Freud's met psychology', *Critical Inquiry*, 13(2), pp. 287–292. Translated by N. Rand.

'Ballarat Wins The Chase', *The Ballarat Courier*, Friday 2 June 2023.

Burkhardt, B. (Editor) (2012) *Conversations with William Maxwell*. Universit Press of Mississippi.

Calvino, I. (2013) *Italian Folk Tales*. Penguin Books.

Camus, A. (1955) *The Myth of Sisyphus and Other Essays*. Translated b J. O'Brien. New York: Vintage.

Cane, S. (2013) 'On this day: First Australian Nobel Prize for Literatur *Australian Geographic*, 13 December. (Quote from Patrick White)

Flanagan, R. (2023) *Question 7*. Penguin Random House.

Fuller, P. (1993) *Henry Moore*. Methuen Publishing.

Grishin, S. (1990) *The Art of John Brack*. Melbourne: Oxford University Pres

Grishin, S. (2017) *Helen Maudsley: In praise of slow art*. Grishin's Art Blog 2 18 November. http://www.sashagrishin.com/blog/archives/11-2017

Kafka, F. (1954) *Letter to His Father*. Translated by E. Kaiser and E. Wilkin New York: Schocken Books.

Kafka, F. (1977) *Letters to Friends, Family, and Editors*. Translated b R. Manheim and E. Muir. New York: Schocken Books, p. 16.

Malcolm, J. (1994) *The Silent Woman: Sylvia Plath and Ted Hughes*. Londo Penguin Books.

Maxwell, W. (1996) *So Long, See You Tomorrow*, Vintage International.

Merwin, W.S. (1983) *Opening The Hand*. New York: Atheneum.

liver, M. (1986) 'The Visitor', *Dream Work*. Boston, MA: Atlantic Monthly ress.

hite, P. (1979) *The Twyborn Affair.* London: Jonathan Cape.

innicott, D.W. (1971) *Playing and Reality*. London: Tavistock Publications.

he image of *The Beach* is a photograph of a reproduction in:
lillar, R. (1971) *John Brack*. Melbourne: Lansdowne Press.

Acknowledgements

Special thanks to my writing group. To Sarah Tomasetti for initiating t group, to Annie Green, Fleur Glenn, Kate Derum, Mary Martin, Ann Drilli and Anna Taylor for responding so generously to my early work, for shari their own writing, and for allowing me to see the possibility of publishi my work.

My deepest gratitude to Anna Rappoport for patiently holding space for to recognise the significance of family secrets, to confront shame, and to gi myself permission to find my own voice.

My sincere thanks to Nadine Davidoff for her superb editing: for seeing wh the book was truly about, for respecting the integrity of the work, and giving me the courage to trust the writing.

To Jenny Kemp, for conversations about being a daughter of artists, and incisive feedback that changed the course of the manuscript.

To Brian Derum, for valuable feedback on early drafts and for his ongoi encouragement.

To Lindsay Brack, for conversations about his childhood with Dad, and his short history of the Brack family.

To Sasha Grishin, for copies of tapes of his interview with Dad for *The A of John Brack*, for references to Mum's work on his blog, *Grishin's Art Bl (GAB)* and for permission to publish his email to me.

To Sarah Sentilles, writing mentor, for inspiring workshops and for enco aging imaginative possibilities in writing.

To Terri-ann White at Upswell Publishing, for her enthusiastic response the pitch of the manuscript and for seeing its potential.

my sisters, Vicky, Freda and Charlotte, for sharing their experiences of ldhood, for offering their perspectives on our parents and for being the ly others in the world who truly *know* them.

ally, to my husband, Ross Williams, and to my daughters, Rose and Alice, their love and for their ongoing support of the quiet work of writing.

About Upswell

Upswell Publishing was established in 2021 by Terri-ann White as a not-for-profit press. A perceived gap in the market for distinctive literary works in fiction, poetry and narrative non-fiction was the motivation. In her years as a bookseller, writer and then publisher, Terri-ann has maintained a watch on literary books and the way they insinuate themselves into a cultural space and are then located within our literary and cultural inheritance. She is interested in making books to last: books with the potential to still be noticed, and noted, after decades and thus be ripe to influence new literary histories.

About this typeface

Book designer Becky Chilcott chose Foundry Origin not only as a strong, carefully considered, and dependable typeface, but also to honour her late friend and mentor, type designer Freda Sack, who oversaw the project. Designed by Freda's long-standing colleague, Stuart de Rozario, much like Upswell Publishing, Foundry Origin was created out of the desire to say something new.

:.ingramcontent.com/pod-product-compliance
:ning Source LLC
rgne TN
W091142080826
145LV00008B/2231